KT-569-329

*To Faim Kibreab
With my admiration
for your research*

Michael Cernee

Cultural Heritage and Development

A Framework for Action in the Middle East and North Africa

 The World Bank

Middle East and North Africa Region

Orientations in Development was launched by the World Bank's Middle East and North Africa Region in 2001 to share analysis of the multifaceted development issues facing the region and to offer practical and innovative solutions. From managing scarce water resources to preserving cultural heritage to enacting policies that promote equitable growth and reduce poverty, the region confronts a broad range of challenges. Each contribution in this series seeks to deepen the knowledge on these topics and enrich the policy debate among development practitioners both within the region and worldwide.

Copyright © 2001 The International Bank for Reconstruction
and Development / THE WORLD BANK
1818 H Street, N.W.
Washington, D.C. 20433, USA

All rights reserved
Manufactured in the United States of America
First printing June 2001
1 2 3 4 03 02 01

The findings, interpretations, and conclusions expressed in this book are entirely those of the authors and should not be attributed in any manner to the World Bank, to its affiliated organizations, or to members of its Board of Executive Directors or the countries they represent. The World Bank does not guarantee the accuracy of the data included in this publication and accepts no responsibility for any consequence of their use. The boundaries, colors, denominations, and other information shown on any map in this volume do not imply on the part of the World Bank Group any judgment on the legal status of any territory or the endorsement or acceptance of such boundaries.

The material in this publication is copyrighted. The World Bank encourages dissemination of its work and will normally grant permission to reproduce portions of the work promptly.

Permission to photocopy items for internal or personal use, for the internal or personal use of specific clients, or for educational classroom use is granted by the World Bank, provided that the appropriate fee is paid directly to the Copyright Clearance Center, Inc., 222 Rosewood Drive, Danvers, MA 01923, USA; telephone 978-750-8400, fax 978-750-4470. Please contact the Copyright Clearance Center before photocopying items.

For permission to reprint individual articles or chapters, please fax a request with complete information to the Republication Department, Copyright Clearance Center, fax 978-750-4470.

All other queries on rights and licenses should be addressed to the Office of the Publisher, World Bank, at the address above or faxed to 202-522-2422.

Cover design by Naylor Design, Inc., Washington, D.C.

ISBN 0-8213-4938-4

Library of Congress Cataloging-in-Publication Data has been applied for.

Contents

Acknowledgements

This strategy research paper on cultural heritage and development was written by Michael M. Cernea, former Senior Adviser for Social Policy of the World Bank, currently Consultant Social Adviser in the Middle East and North Africa Region of the World Bank. The detailed review process that led to it was coordinated by the Social and Economic Department of the Middle East and North Africa (MENA) region, through its Social Team.

Consultations with a large number of government and civil society representatives of MENA countries were carried out for the preparation of this study. The World Bank's regional country teams and sector units closely collaborated in this analysis and shared their experiences. This publication is an abbreviated executive version of the full-length study, devoted to the detailed presentation of MENA region's operational experiences in the cultural sector, which is separately forthcoming in the World Bank's Directions in Development series.

The overall review carried out for this strategy framework paper was guided, during most of its unfolding, by Mustapha K. Nabli, Chief Economist of the MENA Region and Director, Social and Economic Development Group, and, during its initial period, by John Page, currently Director of the Poverty Reduction Group.

The contributions of all those who, in various countries, shared their concerns and recommendations for this report, are gratefully acknowledged. Many thanks are due as well to the United Nations Educational, Scientific, and Cultural Organization (UNESCO) and, in particular, to some of its senior officers—Mounir Bouchenaki, Lamia Salman Al-Madini, and Laurent Levi-Strauss—who helped in the fieldwork for this study. UNESCO's World Heritage Center assisted with reviewing the report and with the maps of World Heritage sites located in MENA countries, for which appreciation is expressed to Francesco Bandarin and Hadi Saliba.

For their comments on earlier drafts and for their contributions of data and insights, thanks are due in particular to A. Al-Khafaji, A. Amahan, M. Albrow, F. Amiot, S. Arif, A. Ben-Achour, P. Bocock, P. Boylan, G. Brizzi, R. Cernea, A. Cohen-Mushlin, C. Delvoie, C. del Castillo, L. de Wulf, S. Davis, K. Duer, M. Fahham, M. Feghoul, A. Fleming, M. Gautier, O. Godron, D. Gressani, S. Hammam, Saadeddin Ibrahim, S. Karam, T. Kolan, N. Krafft, A. Kudat, J. Martin-Brown, B. Narkiss, A. Osman, A. Ouerghi, F. Passacantando, D. Pearce, K. Rennie, M. Rodrigo, S. Sabar, J.-L. Sarbib, I. Serageldin, D. Sewell, E. Shluger, I. Sud, J. Tabaroff, N.L. Tagemouati, J. Villiard, and C. Ward. Their experiences and suggestions have greatly enriched the analysis.

The technical preparation of the various versions of the paper was ably carried out by Ilonka Csekey, with the participation of Mary Lou Gomez, Catherine Guié, Marie Leon, and Gracie Ochieng and was continuously overseen by Jan-Marie Hopkins. Publication design, editing, production, and dissemination were managed by Jennifer Keller for MNSED and by the World Bank's Office of the Publisher.

Foreword

The wealth of cultural heritage endowments of the Middle East and North Africa countries is not only a testament to the importance of the region's contributions to humanity's history. It also represents an enormous capacity to support and inspire the development of the region's countries into the future. On behalf of the Middle East and North Africa (MENA) region of the World Bank, it is with great pride that I present this first volume in our new series, *Orientations in Development.* This volume is devoted specifically to the topic of the region's rich cultural heritage assets, taking stock of the MENA region's activities and experiences in supporting cultural heritage preservation and management, and putting forward options for future action.

The World Bank has increasingly emphasized over the last two decades the need to deliberately and proactively take into account the cultural dimensions of every economic and infrastructural sector within which it works for development. In turn, however, the cultural sector itself requires increased support. Many of the region's innumerable cultural jewels are threatened, in some cases by overuse, in others by neglect, and in many simply by the pressures of economic development and striving toward a better future. The presence of these highly valuable cultural endowments in all the region's countries opens up major opportunities for development, providing a major source of employment, and thereby contributing to the reduction of poverty and the decrease of chronic joblessness.

Cultural heritage preservation is a partnership endeavor, requiring the support and participation of large numbers of interested parties, including governments, donor organizations, and the surrounding population. The World Bank's own interventions must complement, and not duplicate, the many cultural heritage preservation activities ongoing in the region, carried out by a host of partners working in this area, including primarily UNESCO and bilateral donor agencies. For practitioners in the domain of cultural heritage management, this strategy framework is not intended to be a set of rigid prescriptions, but rather to offer an array of operational suggestions. Each situation is different and requires locally tailored solutions and innovative adaptations. The volume emphasizes the need and available options for incorporating cultural heritage management into mainstream development planning and into cross-sectoral approaches.

Proper maintenance and management of the region's cultural heritage assets can positively affect the quality of life through a wealth of channels—economic, cultural, spiritual, and educational. The lessons described within this volume should be considered a starting point for greater attention, increased discussion, and, ultimately, the full protection and use of cultural heritage assets. There is still much to learn with respect to integrating cultural heritage management into development. The Bank's MENA region is poised for further learning. Our actions, and those of others engaged in safeguarding the region's cultural heritage, need to be knitted and embedded in knowledge. Thus, learning continues.

JEAN-LOUIS SARBIB
VICE PRESIDENT
MIDDLE EAST AND NORTH AFRICA REGION

Abbreviations and Acronyms

AKTC	Aga Khan Trust for Culture
APL	Adaptive program lending
CAS	Country assistance strategy
CDF	Comprehensive Development Framework
CH	Cultural heritage
CJA	Center for Jewish Art
CMU	Country management unit
CSERGE	Centre for Social and Economic Research on the Global Environment
CT/CH	Cultural tourism/cultural heritage
CVM	Contingent valuation method
DGF	Development Grant Facility
ERR	Economic rate of return
ESW	Economic and sector work
GDP	Gross domestic product
ICCROM	International Centre for the Study of the Preservation and Restoration of Cultural Property
ICOM	International Council of Museums
ICOMOS	International Council on Monuments and Sites
IDF	Institutional development fund
IFC	International Finance Corporation
ITFCSD	Italian Trust Fund for Culture and Sustainable Development
LIL	Learning and innovation loan
MENA	Middle East and North Africa
MNSED	MENA Social and Economic Department
NGO	Nongovernmental organization
PAD	Project appraisal document
PER	Public expenditure review
PREM	Poverty Reduction and Economic Management (World Bank)

PRSP	Poverty reduction strategy paper
RMT	Regional management team
SDV	Social Development Vice Presidency
UNDP	United Nations Development Programme
UNESCO	United Nations Educational, Scientific, and Cultural Organization
WBI	World Bank Institute
WHL	World Heritage List

Introduction

The countries of the Middle East and North Africa (MENA) are blessed with an extraordinary cultural patrimony, secular and religious, of huge importance for each country and for humankind at large. The region is home to 48 sites already inscribed on the World Heritage List[1] maintained by the United Nations Educational, Scientific, and Cultural Organization (UNESCO) and has an enormous nonmaterial heritage as well (see Box 1). The Middle East is also the cradle of the world's major monotheistic religions. This cultural patrimony is a cornerstone of many people's existence and nourishes their daily lives. It must continue to flourish.

Treasures with vast development potential. The presence of such valuable endowments in all the region's countries opens up a major development opportunity: the cultural patrimony can become a pillar of the region's overall growth-enhancing strategy, as well as a rich foundation for people's education. It can evolve into a source of robust employment, contributing to the reduction of poverty and unemployment. Laudable steps along the lines of this strategy have been taken. Yet much more needs to be done, and exponentially more can be achieved in this domain, for the overall benefit of the region and the world at large.

The treasures of MENA's cultural patrimony, although rich and seemingly inexhaustible, nonetheless suffer from accelerated deterioration and depletion. Many natural, economic, and social processes combine perversely to erode its riches. The cultural patrimony therefore needs increased support for preservation and better management. Development assistance cannot be oblivious to both these opportunities and needs.

Objectives. This paper analyzes the cultural heritage (CH) sector in MENA countries and the World Bank's policy and operational experiences in this sector over the past six years, 1996–2001. It has three objectives:

- To explore the characteristics, capacities, needs, and constraints of the region's cultural sector and their relevance to overall country development

- To take stock, describe, and analyze the World Bank's past and current support for preservation and management of the region's cultural heritage

- To extract the lessons of experience and define the strategy framework for future Bank assistance for preserving and managing the MENA region's patrimony.

As the first regionwide analysis of sectoral issues and Bank-supported cultural heritage (CH) operations, this summary paper can condense only a fraction of the region's accumulated experiences. Those interested in a fuller image and in its empirical documentation are invited to consult the full regional sector review, to be published separately (World Bank forthcoming). This analysis is centered on the material cultural heritage and the historic patrimony's physical endowments.

The study's findings result from field visits; from research on project preparation, appraisal, and implementation; and from economic, finan-

---

BOX 1

UNESCO's Definition of Material Cultural Heritage

The key international document defining cultural heritage is the 1972 UNESCO Convention Concerning the Protection of the World Cultural and Natural Heritage, which has been signed by most governments. Article 1 defines and classifies material CH under three categories:

monuments: *architectural works, works of monumental sculpture and painting, elements or structures of an archaeological nature, inscriptions, cave dwellings and combinations of features which are of outstanding universal value from the point of view of history, art or science;*

groups of buildings: *groups of separate or connected buildings which, because of their architecture, their homogeneity or their place in the landscape, are of outstanding universal value from the point of view of history, art or science;*

sites: *works of man or the combined works of nature and man, and areas including archaeological sites which are of outstanding value from the historical, aesthetic, ethnological or anthropological point of view.*

This definition of material cultural heritage has been broadened in the scholarly literature after 1972, so as to cover not only monumental items but also movable-heritage goods, such as collections in museums, works of art, and movable antiquities.

cial, and risk analyses for projects with CH components. For the preparation of this regionwide framework study, policy consultations were organized with the governments of several MENA countries; with UNESCO, the United Nations Development Programme (UNDP), several donor countries, and various international and national institutions; and with local communities and nongovernmental organizations (NGOs) that deal with culture. Their valuable recommendations for MENA's strategy are incorporated into this report.

Past neglect. In the past, narrow development models have overlooked the importance of cultural dimensions in inducing and managing development, underestimating the intrinsic economic capacity of the cultural sector for empowering development. Like many national governments, the World Bank has bypassed many of the sector's issues and needs. Despite some exceptions (for example, the successful rehabilitation of old Hafsia, in Tunis, under an urban development project), the economic resources of the cultural patrimony have been seldom mobilized; generally they have not been taken into account in the Bank's economic and social analyses or assistance strategies. In 1980, for instance, the Bank decided to cease lending for tourism, including cultural tourism—a measure that reduced its limited support for patrimony management as well.[2] Today, overcoming such biases is a premise for incorporating new sociocultural potentials into country strategies and Bank programs.

Country needs and demands. During the past five to six years, several MENA country governments have increasingly called on the World Bank to assist in addressing the needs of the cultural sector, particularly for:

- Linking urban and tourism investment projects with direct support for heritage preservation

- Safeguarding endangered patrimony assets in ways that incorporate them into development strategies and yield economic and social benefits

- Expanding the institutional capacity for managing these national resources.

Changes in development thinking. The increased recognition now being given to culture is part of the broader changes that have taken place in development thinking in the 1990s generally. Today, the World Bank is promoting a more encompassing development paradigm, as outlined in the Comprehensive Development Framework (CDF), which places the inducement of economic growth within its *social* context (see Wolfensohn 1999b). This is why the Bank now recognizes, and advances the idea, that the cultural sector contributes to effective economic growth rather than just consuming budgetary resources. Furthermore, development assistance is not a narrow pursuit of economic growth alone but aims at broad social development. Culture and cultural heritage cannot be left out of development assistance programs. The Bank's deepening grasp of what makes nations prosper leads, among other initiatives, to including investments for culture in development lending.

This thinking firmly places support for CH within the broader map of MENA's development strategy. From this overall perspective, assistance for cultural heritage is practiced neither as an activity separate from regular development work nor as a conjectural add-on to "business as usual" (Sarbib 2000). Instead, it is conceived as intrinsic to affirmation of the region's identity, development orientation, and philosophy, to be pursued in unity with the countries' and the Bank's basic objectives of poverty reduction, economic reform, and political participation. "The future of the Middle East and North Africa will be determined by progress on economic reform, political participation and *the cultivation of a strong identity rooted in the region's history but open to the rest of the world*" (Dervis and Shafik 1998: 505; emphasis added).

The rationale for including CH preservation in regular development programs holds that development as a goal can and must be pursued through cultural endowments means as well, in addition to other means. Conversely, the goal of patrimony preservation must be pursued with the means offered by development and modern management, rather than through traditional conservation only.

This development rationale also rests on the proposition that culture is not just a commodity, not just another rank-and-file economic resource. Because the patrimony's value is multifaceted—cultural, moral, spiritual, political, and economic—investing in it is justified by the worthy goals of nation building and cultural self-preservation, as well as by the capacity of CH to be a powerful engine of economic development.

Pioneering projects. To implement this orientation, the Bank's MENA region is developing a pioneering set of investment projects in the cultural heritage sectors of Jordan, Lebanon, Morocco, Tunisia, West Bank–Gaza, and other areas. The region also provides nonlending assistance in this domain in Algeria, the Arab Republic of Egypt, the Islamic Republic of Iran, the Syrian Arab Republic, West Bank–Gaza, and Yemen, among others. The ongoing work supporting cultural heritage is varied; it consists of investment projects or project components for patrimony management, heritage inventories, small-scale community activities, studies, and other initiatives. That stock of pioneering experiences, analyzed in this report, is the basis on which countries and the Bank can build their further cooperation in the CH domain.

Learning continues. The region's CH assistance strategy is a work in progress. Learning continues. Many issues require further research and thinking. Moreover, the cultural domain includes both the region's historic cultural heritage and the innumerable ongoing cultural activities in contemporary arts, literature and music, theater and dance, and so on. Given the breadth of the domain, this strategy study concentrates on the Bank's support for the region's vast material (built) heritage of national and universal value, as defined by UNESCO and by relevant international agreements (see Box 1). The review discusses policy, institutional, and management issues, operational project design options, economic and social benefits, and risk and financing issues and outlines recommendations.

Because some countries are not yet accustomed to the Bank's playing an assistance role in the CH domain, the MENA region expects to encounter a substantial need for information, as well as new questions and challenges, during its further interaction with governments and with all stakeholders. Strategy dialogues will therefore continue at all relevant levels: with central organizations (ministries of culture, finance, tourism, artisanat, education, environment, and so on), with regional and local authorities, and with civil society and the business sector. The Bank's MENA region actively invites further proposals to fine-tune and enrich its strategy and activities.

Iron Age pots excavated in the United Arab Emirates.

Islamic architecture, the dominant feature in the cultural landscape of the MENA region, is intertwined with the material testimonies left by pre-Islamic civilizations. In Marrakesh, the Minaret of the Koutoubia Mosque (the Mosque of the Booksellers), originally constructed in the 11th century by the Almoravid dynasty, is now embraced by the scaffoldings of its ongoing restoration (top). Innumerable houses of learning, the medersas, often harbor intricate decorations, such as the ornate Medrassa Es Sahrij, in Fès. In Jordan, Jerash (bottom), as in many other places, remains of Roman, Greek, Egyptian, and other civilizations preserve the cultures of prior populations.

CHAPTER 1

The Cultural Sector in MENA Countries

Culture in development. Cultural dimensions, like economic dimensions, are naturally present in every human endeavor and development process, not only in special "cultural development" programs. From this premise, it follows that an *explicit recognition* of these cultural dimensions must be incorporated into the formulation of all development policies and project interventions.

The recognition of culture, and its deliberate incorporation into induced development, involve two requirements. First, it requires identification and awareness of the cultural dimensions in all development interventions in the so-called *non*cultural sectors. This is indispensable because sensitivity to cultures enables development projects to fit better into their contexts, energizes stakeholders, and facilitates participation. Second, incorporation requires that sociocultural knowledge be used in the key processes for inducing development, such as policy formulation, planning, financing, and institutional mobilization. Meeting these two requirements increases the sustainability of development by grounding it in each country's culture.

Recognition of the place of culture in development would be incomplete, however, if only the cultural dimensions of *non*cultural sectors were addressed, without direct support for the cultural sector itself. These are two sides of the same mainstreaming philosophy. Together, they achieve synergy. Since the first aspect has been treated in many previous documents (see Cernea 1991), this analysis addresses the cultural sector itself and focuses on patrimony issues.

Below, we briefly characterize the extraordinary riches of MENA's cultural heritage endowments as a huge collection of assets testifying to a mosaic of civilizations. However difficult and incomplete such a summary inevitably is, the overview will suggest the complexities of the task of managing the patrimony.[2] Further, the analysis will focus on the threats to the patrimony's sustainability and the perverse convergence of natural, economic, and social causes that results in accelerated deterioration.

The Sector: Actors, Assets, Industries, and Institutions

The cultural sector. For the purposes of this paper, the working concept of "cultural sector" or "patrimony sector" is used to connote and to encompass several elements that, taken together, are defined as a sector. These constitutive elements are:

A. *Specific assets:* cultural patrimony endowments

B. *Industries and productive activities:* cultural industries, including traditional artisanal enterprises

C. *Service activities and organizations:* organized structures for facilitating public access to heritage, such as museums, libraries, theaters, exhibitions, and cultural tourism companies

D. *Commercial enterprises:* shops, formal and informal markets for culturally related artifacts, artisanal products, and the like

E. *Institutions:* a set of state institutions, as well as semigovernmental and nongovernmental organizations dedicated to work on patrimony conservation and management.

A brief overview of the constitutive elements of the sector, and of the challenges and constraints the sector faces in MENA countries, follows.

Actors and challenges. The current major challenges to the patrimony must be seen as challenges to all actors working in the cultural sector. These actors are numerous and varied; they range from administrators directly responsible for safekeeping and managing the sector's treasures to the legions of artists and artisans who perpetuate heritage traditions, from those employed in cultural industries and service organizations to those laboring in the sector's institutions or as creative artists on their own. But in a larger sense, the actors are all the country's citizens who enjoy, admire, and use their heritage, and the nations themselves, which have the responsibility for preserving, perpetuating, and transmitting the heritage.

The nations of the Middle East and North Africa now confront two central challenges to their extraordinary patrimony. The first is weak management and the disconnect between patrimony and development, which preempt the adequate capture of the patrimony's vast economic and educational values. Second, the material patrimony is threatened by growing risks of deterioration and accelerating loss.

A. The Patrimony's Assets: A Mosaic of Civilizations

The cultural heritage endowments of the region are usually classified under three large categories:

- Archaeological and historical sites, monuments, and collections
- Urban and rural ensembles such as the built medinas and kasbahs
- Living cultural heritage: folklife and folklore, traditional arts and crafts, and related elements.

Regional geography has framed history and political developments. What in the World Bank vernacular is called "the MENA region" represents a geographically vast mosaic of several distinct past civilizations and the contemporary societies that are their heirs. The region encompasses a plurality of nations, and an even greater number of ethnic and culturally diverse groups. The vast movements of its populations, the ever-expanding trade routes, the wars and political conquests, the rise and collapse of empires and states, the juxtaposition of civilizations, explain the diversity and pluralism of the region's heritage.

The region can trace the history of its civilizations to more than 11,000 years ago, with the earliest Paleolithic hunting implements discovered in the caves of Mount Carmel. Jericho's multistrata site reveals cultural evidence dating back some 9,000 years, when the area was occupied by Mesolithic peoples. In the Fertile Crescent of Mesopotamia, in the fourth millennium B.C.E., Neolithic and Chalcolithic settlements were replaced by the Sumerian civilization, which was itself nearly destroyed about 2500 B.C.E. by Semitic tribes from the Arabian Desert. Akkad, the mighty city that arose on the ruins of Sumer, was displaced by Assyrian, Babylonian, and Persian civilizations. Amorites from the west, the Indo-European Hittites from central Asia, Arameans, Phoenicians, Hebrews, Philistines, Greeks, Romans, Turks, Mongols, Arabs, and, much later, the French, the English, and many others—all have left their mark on the Middle East. To the west, the fertile Nile valley sheltered during this long history a series of civilizations that raised the gigantic Egyptian pyramids and built Luxor's unique temples.

The seafaring Phoenicians first extended Middle East trade and influence throughout the entire Mediterranean area, reaching the Atlantic Ocean by the second millennium B.C.E. Settlements such as Volubilis in Morocco, which reveal complex societies and trading activities, testify to the extent of Phoenician and then Roman power and influence. With their victory over the Phoenicians in 211 B.C.E. at Carthage, the Romans gained mastery over the entire Mediterranean area, and Roman colonies prospered across North Africa. Palmyra in Syria and Timgad in Algeria (now, like Carthage, on the World Heritage List) are among the most representative towns of those times, miraculously preserved for today's and tomorrow's generations.

The seventh century of the current era marked the beginning of the Islamic period, which enormously enriched the area's culture, material civilization, political forms, and artistic expressions. Islamic and Arab architecture wrote a new chapter in the patrimony of the region and the world. Islamic culture, resting on many prior layers of embedded history, remains the dominant culture of the area to this date (Serageldin 1996). After the 15th century and the consolidation of Christian power in Iberia, exiles and migrants from southern Iberia brought Andalusian art, together with their unique style of life, to North Africa. Jewish communities, old in the area, gradually grew large within the medinas and became widespread throughout the region, especially from the 15th century to the mid-20th century. The commonalities, as well as the differences, in the structures of the houses of worship of the three monotheistic religions (Narkiss 2001) express once again the inner linkages in the region's mutually influenting cultures.

Volubilis, Morocco, a former Roman provincial capital, now a World Heritage site, has striking mosaics, colonnades, houses, public buildings, olive presses, and craftsmen's shops. However, the site lacks resources for building a visitors' center and display rooms: very precious Punic, Roman, and Hebrew tablets are piled up unprotected on improvised shelves.

Perhaps the most concise characterization that can be given of MENA culturally is that it is nothing less than a vast archive of the history of several Western and Eastern civilizations. Richly beautified by humankind's creativity and its built settlements, the region is home to 48 sites inscribed on the World Heritage List (WHL) to date.[2] (See the names and locations of these sites on the maps at the end of this volume.) For comparison, by mid-2000 there were 32 World Heritage sites inscribed in East Asia, 31 in South Asia, 20 in Sub-Saharan Africa, and 41 in Latin America and the Caribbean. The World Heritage List[1] merely indicates, but does not exhaust, the enormous cultural wealth lying visible or hidden in the region's sands, in its cities, and in the memories and lifestyles of its peoples. Many experts agree that the MENA region's cultural riches are still underrepresented and that numerous sites not yet on the list are equal in value, beauty, and significance.

It is impossible now, in fact, to accurately quantify the sheer magnitude of the patrimony in MENA because the work of inventorying it is still going on, is incomplete, or, in some countries, such as Yemen, has not even begun in earnest. Tunisia, for instance, has 8 sites on the WHL, but a preliminary and incomplete "archaeological map" lists over 21,000 sites (ICCROM 1996). The West Bank is reported to contain at least 1,600 archaeological sites (UNESCO/Palestinian Authority 1998). In addition to its 8 WHL-certified sites, Morocco has identified over 15,000 sites and historic monuments. It has classified 243 prehistoric rock-art sites of exceptional value, out of about 17,000 such sites that are known to exist. Resource scarcity restricts governments from granting a "classified" status and protection regime to more monuments and sites. That also reduces their ability to capture the economic potential of many exceptional monuments.

World religions. Judaism, Christianity, and Islam, the three major monotheistic world religions, had their birthplaces in the area encompassed today by MENA and remain an essential part of the region's and all humanity's heritage. Religious communities have built shrines of universal spiritual meanings. The old walled city of Jerusalem embodies within one unique urban environment the roots and links of these three religions. The holiest shrines are here: the Western Wall of Solomon's Temple, the Church of the Holy Sepulchre, and the Al-Aqsa Mosque, with the Dome of the Rock, as well as numerous other sites and buildings of profound spiritual significance. Empires were established under religious flags. Armies moving from east to west or from west to east carried not only their weaponry but also deep cultural influences (Braudel 1966). The ideas, beliefs, and values and the archaeological treasures stemming from those times—holy sites, shrines, madrassas, manuscripts, tombs, forts, and so on—claim today the loyalties of innumerable people throughout the world.

Medieval and modern urban spaces: the medinas. Medinas are a particular type of medieval Islamic city, present in every country in the Maghreb and the Mashreq. They are important not only for their built physical structures but also for their typical social fabric that today cannot be replicated but could be, one can hope, preserved. With their labyrinthine alleys and souks, these ancient walled cities seem lifted from the pages of medieval history books—but for their inhabitants and artisans, they are still the normal way of life. Most dramatic are the old cities of Yemen, such as Shibam and Zabid, with their tall brown mud towerhouses outlined in white plaster, now slowly abandoned by the young who go to find work outside, near or far. At the other end of the Mediterranean are the medinas of Essaouira, Fès, and Marrakesh and the imperial cities of Meknes, Tetouan, and Tunis. Ancient Damascus, Bosra, and Aleppo, the kasbah of Algiers, and the Old Town of Ghadames in Libya are also on the World Heritage List.

The built heritage in rural areas. Rural areas, in turn, have their specific types of built heritage. The fortification architecture of the Maghreb, for instance, reflects patterns of ancient social organization and collective defense. Most typical are the kasbah, the family compound with the appearance of a fortress, and the qsar, the fortified village containing several kasbahs. Tombs of holy men (kubbas) scattered in the rural landscapes have become important pilgrimage places, but their maintenance is endangered by severe competition for land.

Belated systematic research. To many, it may be a surprise to learn that broad awareness of the value of this inestimable heritage and scientific attempts to preserve it came rather late. Archaeological expeditions started only around the end of the 18th century and the beginning of the 19th century. The first archaeologists exported their finds outside the region, to museums in London, Paris, and Berlin and to private collections. Only in the past five to six decades have scholars from developing countries joined such systematic investigations in substantial numbers. This research and inventorying work needs much stronger national and international support than is now accorded it.

New discoveries. Altogether, the cultural heritage of the Middle Eastern and North African countries—a vast thesaurus only palely outlined above—defies any finite description. New discoveries continue to enrich the known heritage. The wealth of the underwater cultural her-

Buried in the sand of the Syrian desert until 1950, the 2nd century Roman theater exemplifies the glory of Palmyrian architecture. Northwest of the site, traditional "beehive houses" in rural areas are inhabited to this day.

itage is only now beginning to be uncovered, as underwater archaeological research is just starting. Stunning examples of the treasures that are still hidden are the recent finds at Tel Ibrahim Awad on the muddy flatlands of the Nile River Eastern Delta, where several temples from about 3200 B.C.E. have been unearthed (Gugliotta 2000). These shed light on Egypt's little-known predynastic period, when King Narmer unified Upper and Lower Egypt and established the pharaonic dynasties that ruled the country for nearly three millennia. Their original architecture is different from anything known anywhere else.[3] The undiscovered parts of this region's heritage surely still hold great surprises for the world at large.

Living culture. Throughout MENA, there is also an enduring and rich oral cultural heritage, complementing the written and the built heritages. Traditional music, popular crafts, folklore, oral histories, dances, story-telling, customs, and ways of life—all are unique instances of living culture and are an intrinsic part of the area's cultural heritage. Djemaal el Fna Square in Marrakesh, Morocco, and the large souk in Old Sana'a, Yemen, are outstanding examples of living cultural heritage treasures with which few, if any, other places in the world could compare. But they are also precious in a financial sense to the artisans and small business-men who fill the open space with artisanal merchandise, food stands, and souvenir shops and with musical or theatrical performances.

To sum up a domain that defies any attempt at a summary, the physical and intangible treasures that form MENA's cultural patrimony are of incalculable value for the present and future of these countries. In the simplest possible terms, it is this value and irreplaceability that together call for exploring their relevance for development. Preservation of this multicultural archive is part of the preservation of humanity's cultural pluralism—preservation of both commonalities and diversity, neither at the expense of the other. "Multiculturalism is the normal human experience" (Goodenough 1987).

B. Cultural Industries and Productive Activities

The artisanat and the cultural industries hold important weight in the MENA countries' cultural sectors and national economies. Through the hands and spirits of uncounted generations of craftsmen, many creations of the past continue to be creations of the present, as well. Much contemporary handicraft production represents another, and very important, living embodiment of the region's cultural heritage. Handicrafts combine traditional folk arts and a rich body of know-how and old technologies with old or renewed decorative patterns. The diversity of products—responding to national and international demands—is enormous, from the silver jewelry of the Middle East to Morocco's pottery and ceramics, from Iranian carpets to Egyptian stone carvings, from wooden objects for daily use to the splendor of multicolored silk and cotton fabrics, from leather items to artistic or utilitarian blown-glass objects, from gleaming brass pots to reconstructed traditional musical instruments or unique architectural and masonry decorations. These products often attain very high levels of refinement and craftsmanship (Maarouf 1999). Their chances of perpetuation in the future are weak, unless this part of the inherited popular culture survives competition with modern techniques and is helped to coexist with serial production on conveyor belts.

Living traditional arts and crafts, however, are also important economically, as a large industry within which millions and millions of people, grouped in medium-size enterprises and microworkshops, are earning their daily living. In Morocco alone, for instance, about 2 million people are now working in the artisanal subsector. They represent about 12 percent of Morocco's active population and contribute close to 10 percent of its gross domestic product (GDP). Falsifying the many somber predictions about the end of the road for handicraft industries, in Fès, for instance, a recent study found that 60 percent of the town's 5,800 artisanal units are relatively new: they were established in the 1980s and 1990s (Tagemouati 2001). About 33 percent of Morocco's artisanal exports consists of carpets and about 20 percent, of pottery. Producers of traditional carpets and kilims in the countries of Muslim culture both perpetuate and

Moroccan artisans, heirs to ancient traditions, enrich the old patterns and create create marvels of engraved brass and copper.

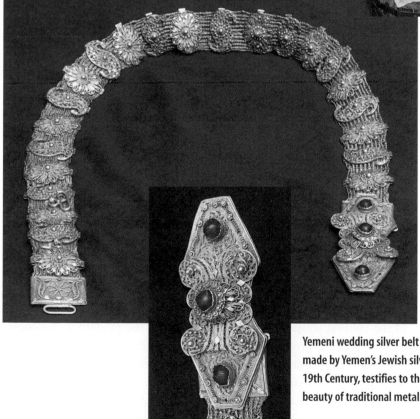

Yemeni wedding silver belt and belt buckle, made by Yemen's Jewish silversmiths in the 19th Century, testifies to the creativity and beauty of traditional metal arts.

develop the heritage by introducing continuous changes in design and in the techniques applied (IRCICA 1999).

C. Cultural Commercial Enterprises

Commercial enterprises that specialize in heritage goods employ a vast number of people. Unfortunately, sectoral and subsectoral statistics are lacking, and it is difficult to determine the relative weight of all cultural enterprises and the labor force they employ.

Partial studies available in some countries indicate that the weight of commercial enterprises related to cultural heritage, in the context of MENA's national economies and labor markets, is substantial. Yet weak marketing fails to fully realize the economic value of the goods that are commercialized. There is ample room to enhance their competitiveness; broaden the enterprises' access to national and foreign markets; and increase their productivity, trade volumes and revenue. This, in turn, will expand the cultural sector's contribution to growth, poverty reduction, and development.

D. Service Organizations and Museums

The service organizations designed to act as "transmission belts" between the patrimony and its interested publics are integral to the cultural sector. Cultural tourism organizations are a key provider (Berriane 1997; see also Ibrahim and Ghorbel 1995). At this juncture, effective interaction between state cultural agencies, religious cultural institutions, and private tourism businesses is more critical for success than in many other domains. Yet this review has found, in country after country, many unresolved issues concerning regulatory jurisdiction over assets, lack of operational cooperation, inequitable sharing of costs and benefits. Dysfunctionalities in this sphere vary from one country to the next. Regionwide, this "node" demands vast improvements. A more supportive business environment is necessary, together with catalytic financial sector services.

Museum networks in MENA countries are ages behind the richness of the cultural patrimony itself, and behind in the modern technologies of preservation, presentation, and public education. Evidence for this conclusion is provided by the analysis for the present report and by many museographers from Algeria, Bahrain, Jordan, Morocco, Oman, Qatar, the United Arab Emirates, and other MENA countries (Al Abouddi 1994; Al Far, Al Jabar, and assoc., 1994; Bouabdellah 1994; Al Sindi 1994). Privately established museums, in turn, receive little state encouragement, although some of them, such as Rabat's large and privately created Belghazi Museum, have amply demonstrated their capacity and use-fulness.[4] Museums are at the very heart of the cultural services networks because they shelter public goods and offer them to public view. The development of a network of national, regional, and community-based museums, complemented by privately owned museums, all with collectors' support, is among the most critical institutional needs in MENA countries. Some, such as Morocco, lack and need to create a national museum or national library.

One other type of service organization largely missing regionwide in the Middle East and North Africa (with rare exceptions, as in Tunisia), is the *mise en valeur* kind of agency. Such agencies are structured to manage and oversee the daily use of and access to patrimony assets, for safeguarding and for revenue generation. Establishing many such specialized management organizations would fill an important gap. Currently, inefficient administrative procedures and outdated technical equipment leave numerous patrimony assets simply unmanaged. The assets deteriorate, out of sight and care. The largest part of MENA's patrimony is not, at present, even inventoried and classified. It is hard to manage what is not well counted. Successful practice in Tunisia has shown that this type of functional management agency substantially increases both access to culture and revenues.[5]

E. Sector Institutions and Governance Patterns

Last but not least, the cultural sector includes the scaffolding of public institutions to which the state entrusts the responsibility for patrimony administration, safeguarding, and management. MENA countries differ widely as to the ministerial body in which patrimony management is legally vested. The Maghreb countries all have ministries of culture that are separate from their ministries of tourism.[6] By contrast, Mashreq countries have more than one pattern, and patrimony management is sometimes included in the ministry of tourism rather than in the ministry of culture.[7] Beyond the variations from country to country, weak organization for managing patrimony assets is a frequent characteristic.[8]

Religious institutions. An important MENA particularity is that ownership and management of a vast segment of the patrimony is under the ministries of the Habous and Islamic affairs and ministries of the Waqf. These assets include both religious buildings (mosques, madrassas, churches, synagogues, libraries, and monuments) and secular buildings such as historic palaces, traditional caravanseries, and residential housing. Despite their sacred character, some of the religious properties are chronically poorly maintained and in bad physical condition.

From this dual or plural nature of asset ownership emerges a host of institutional and budgetary implications. The state and the civil society expect the religious institutions to improve their self-management capacity, exercise their upkeep duties over this segment of the national patrimony, and allocate from their distinct revenues the amounts necessary. Strengthening institutional capacity countrywide requires improved governance by the religious institutions of the built heritage. Increased institutional cooperation between religious entities and state agencies is a prerequisite for success.

The institutional assessment of the CH sector in MENA countries reveals chronic constraints that vary from country to country, but obvious commonalities surface. Capacity needs appear throughout the three constitutive elements of governance: policy, organization, and financing.

The Umayyad Mosque (Damascus, Syria), one of the world's largest mosques: grand courtyard, with 8th century Kubbet Al-Khazneh, or Dome of the Treasure (left), and 18th century Kubbet al-Saa, or Dome of the Hours (center).

● *Policy vacuums.* The cultural patrimony of MENA countries is protected by legal regulations, but proactive policies focused on management and links with development are rarely in place. Where such policies exist, as in Egypt and in the case of Tunisia's pioneering Code du Patrimoine, the positive impacts are obvious. Some laws are old (in Lebanon, they date from 1933) and are insufficiently responsive to the complex needs of modern preservation and development. Legal regulations for protecting assets against encroachment, destruction, and theft are not systematically enforced through systems of incentives

and penalties. In response to an UNESCO survey, government officials in most Arab countries expressed the strong belief that a general
reform of CH policies and laws is needed (UNESCO, World Heritage
Committee 2000).

- *Organizational weaknesses.* At the center, ministries of culture tend to
be understaffed and underfinanced. Cross-sectoral cooperation with
other sectors and ministries is sporadic—piecemeal rather than strategic—and the financing allocations received (see further) are meager.
UNESCO's World Heritage Committee recently noted that the heritage services—despite demonstrated will to execute their tasks, often
under difficult circumstances—are ill equipped and lack staff, skills,
materials, and funding. These services appear to suffer from a lack of
integration of their activities into a wider development approach. If
they were so integrated, they might have easier access to the development means that are now not available to them (UNESCO, World
Heritage Committee 2000). Weaknesses in realizing the patrimony's
potential are hampering related economic activities, as well.

Analysis reveals that *decentralization* to regional and municipal
authorities is only incipient, at best. The management of CH assets
cannot be carried out from the capital city only. Much of the material
patrimony is located in small or medium-size localities, which do not
yet possess (and are not being given) the resources required to maintain and manage major heritage assets. The typical discrepancy—
definable as "small community–big heritage"—is not counteracted
adequately. Weak capacity at local levels, in turn, deprives the national centers of organizational depth. With some country variations,
these institutions tend to be center-heavy and thin at the periphery.

Traditional musical instruments, still in use in various
areas of the Maghreb.

Institutional weakness also results from the absence of a social con-
tract between government structures and the structures of civil society, for participation of the latter in CH management and in containing the natural, economic, and social causes of patrimony loss. The
vast reservoirs of energy and initiative of the population at large and
of the business sector are still to be activated and motivated toward
regular civic engagement in CH.

- *Low financing levels.* In almost all MENA countries, the share of the
ministry of culture in the national budget currently ranks at the bottom of the investment totem pole. Table 1.1 reflects the absolute
amounts spent in MENA countries (in U.S. dollars) and the ratios of
culture-related expenditures to national GDP over the period
1986–98. With the exception of Egypt, this ratio is currently below 1
percent and in several countries is below 0.5 percent. Even these low
levels do not yet reveal the full story of underfinancing, because the

data in Table 1.1 are aggregates: they include expenditures not just for culture but also for sports and religious affairs. Available statistics do not offer a breakdown of these expenditures, but the fraction for culture is clearly small. For instance, in the case of Yemen, Table 1.1 reports that in 1998 cultural expenditures accounted for 1 percent of GDP, but a public expenditure review (PER) undertaken by the World Bank in 2000 found that only about one-tenth of the 1 percent went for culture and that nine-tenths was used for sports and religious affairs (de Wulf 2001). More or less comparable proportions can be assumed for the other MENA countries. The allocations for the cultural sector by itself, and specifically for CH, are much lower than the percentages shown in this table—with obvious consequences.

The rationale for these extremely limited allocations invites serious reconsideration.[9] The prevailing resource scarcity also calls for more energetic mobilization of nongovernment funds.

External support. This sectoral study found that over the past 10 to 15 years, external financial support from United Nations bodies for CH preservation projects has been limited. These grants, which, on average, are rather small per project, were able to meet some immediate emergencies, but they were not designed for comprehensive, large-scale sec-

TABLE 1.1

Culture-Related Expenditures in MENA Countries and Ratios to GDP, Selected Years, 1986–98

(millions of U.S. dollars for amounts; percent for ratio of cultural expenditures to GDP)

Country	1986		1990		1992		1994		1996		1997		1998	
	Amt.	Ratio	Amt.	Ratio	Amt.	Ratio	Amt.	Ratio	Amt.	Ratio	Amt.	Ratio	Amt.	Ratio
Bahrain	20.2	0.6	25.0	0.6	28.7	0.6	26.9	0.5	9.8	0.2	27.9	0.5	31.4	..
Egypt, Arab Rep. of	1013.1	2.8	852.6	2.2	978.0	2.0	1394.1	2.4	1653.0	..	1865.6	..	..	..
Iran, Islamic Rep. of	670.2	0.3	410.1	0.3	433.3	0.4	388.3	0.5	714.8	0.8	880.0	0.9	950.5	..
Israel	123.7	0.4	234.1	0.4	349.7	0.5	324.8	0.4	469.0	0.5	455.4	0.5	435.8	..
Jordan	46.8	0.8	22.2	0.6	24.6	0.5	39.9	0.7	55.6	0.8	49.8	..	..	..
Kuwait	189.3	1.1	222.2	1.2	245.4	1.2	370.4	1.5	307.3	1.0	323.1	1.1	414.5	..
Malta	4.6	0.4	17.9	0.8	21.6	0.8	19.3	0.7	20.6	0.6	29.8	0.9	..	..
Morocco	24.8	0.1	42.1	0.2	61.7	0.2	99.5	0.3	..	..	..	..	..	..
Oman	97.9	1.3	89.7	0.9	133.9	1.2	125.1	1.1	108.2	0.7	92.8	0.6	93.1	..
Syrian Arab Rep.	67.7	0.5	44.2	0.4	44.5	0.3	58.5	0.4	61.3	0.4	62.7	..	..	..
Tunisia	80.6	0.9	99.7	0.8	144.6	0.9	157.4	1.0	172.3	0.9	..	..	..	..
Yemen	..	..	27.9	0.6	42.1	0.8	26.9	0.8	33.2	0.6	43.7	0.8	51.6	1.0
United Arab Emirates	95.9	0.4	100.5	0.3	133.8	0.4	135.7	0.4	..	..	..	..	..	..

Notes: Cultural expenditures are taken from IMF, Government Financial Statistics, various years. Line B8 (Recreational, Cultural and Religious Affairs), Budgetary Central Government. GDP information is from Live Database as of June 23, 1999.

toral interventions. There is certainly a need for more substantial external support, perhaps in new forms, to developing countries that act as custodians and managers of patrimony endowments and thus provide cultural services of international benefit. Substantial bilateral aid has been and is being provided to MENA countries by industrial countries, primarily but not exclusively by those with historical cultural links to the Mediterranean area, including Italy, France, Japan, Spain, Germany, the United Kingdom, and others. A consensus is slowly emerging that improved international cooperation and cofinancing arrangements could enhance the volume of patrimony-oriented development aid (Commission on Global Governance 1995).

To sum up, the review of the sector's component "building blocks" in MENA countries—assets, industries, commercial enterprises, services, and institutions—reveals a vast, diversified, and complex domain, central to the life of these societies and with an important place in their economies. The most important current challenge to the sector is to strengthen its institutional structures, overcome governance weaknesses, link to development's mainstream, and reform the management and financing of the sector.

Loss of Patrimony Treasures: Causes and Needs

The second major challenge to the heritage thesaurus in MENA countries is its accelerated deterioration. Cultural heritage is under threat. Under the impact of relentless natural factors and of even worse damages induced by people-caused processes, much is being lost forever. This is the most severe risk facing the patrimony—a risk that requires in-depth understanding and concerted responses.

Perishability of patrimony assets. It is true that the loss of material heritage is not a novel occurrence. What is new is that recent economic circumstances combine dangerously with natural causes to increase the magnitude and speed of this destruction, with irreparable consequences for present and future generations. The material heritage is a perishable public good, and states and nations have a compelling responsibility for preserving it.

National governments in MENA countries, civil societies, and UNESCO and the international community have repeatedly sounded the alarm bell about this deteriorating situation. Because the "development perspective" advocates a role for the patrimony as a resource for development, it is incumbent upon it to also address the formidable problems of stemming the loss of patrimony.

Causes of patrimony loss. What are the major risks, losses, and constraints in MENA countries that currently endanger CH preservation? What has the Bank's MENA region done to assist governments in addressing these risks and constraints? A synthesis of case studies and country documents concerning patrimony deterioration, sheer robbery, or wanton destruction indicates that four clusters of causes are at work:

(a) Natural causes
(b) Economic causes
(c) Social causes
(d) Institutional weaknesses.

In Saudi Arabia, Jeddah's old traditional houses are famous for their latticed woodwork and original architecture, but many are in need of restoration.

Natural causes. Although natural causes of deterioration have long been recognized, protection lags far behind today's level of knowledge about possible preventive action. Natural disasters such as earthquakes, floods, major storms, and landslides, as well as regular natural processes—time itself and its merciless effects, rainfall, wind, and temperature changes—all slowly sap the resilience of ancient physical monuments or buildings, increase their vulnerability, and then destroy them during dramatic events.

A characteristic of the built heritage of MENA countries is its concentration in coastal areas along the Mediterranean shores (see the maps at the end of the report). Their geographic location implies constant exposure to high humidity and coastal erosion. In turn, the erosion may be partly natural and partly caused by human action, through intensive coastal zone development. In addition, tall buildings and minarets are highly vulnerable to seismic events (Crocci 1997). As Box 1.1 shows, a considerable part of the built heritage of MENA countries has been devastated by disastrous earthquakes over the centuries (Abouseif 1994). Poor husbandry of the domestic water supply and, often, the absence of drainage combine to increase humidity and decay and to accelerate the crumbling of historic buildings.

Economic causes. Compounding adverse natural conditions, economic growth itself unleashes a set of economic causes of deterioration of the heritage.

- *Infrastructure construction* can lead to extensive losses during the building of highways, roads, railways and airports, hydropower dams and reservoirs, new towns and industrial estates, and mines. Infrastructure required for urban expansion accounts for major losses in Cairo, Carthage, Sana'a, and many other old cities.

- *Economic and technological changes* have gradually pushed out many traditional crafts and wares from old medinas and souks, modifying pro-

---

BOX 1.1

Earthquake Disasters and the Built Heritage

Irreparable losses have been inflicted throughout the centuries to the cultural patrimony in MENA countries by earthquakes, floods, and other natural calamities. Risk of further damage from earthquakes requires preventive reinforcement of the most endangered historic buildings and monuments to help them withstand future calamities.

- *Agadir,* Morocco's historic western port on the Atlantic Ocean, was devastated in 1960 by two consecutive earthquakes; about 15,000 people died. Rebuilding of the city began shortly thereafter, but most of its monuments cannot be reconstructed. Large parts of the historic city were leveled, and the cultural site is lost.

- Algeria's major urban center, *Orleansville* (renamed El-Asnam and then Chleff), which had been affected by earthquakes in 1905, 1922, and 1928, was destroyed in 1954 and again in 1980 by major earthquakes. Many unprotected historic and religious buildings have been lost, particularly during the last two earthquakes.

- *Beirut* and its famous law school were destroyed by the big earthquake of the sixth century C.E., which also badly damaged Baalbek's monumental temples.

- In *Egypt,* more than 30 earthquakes were registered between 796 and 1500 C.E. In 1847 a single earthquake destroyed 42 mosques in El Fayoum. In the 1992 Dahshour earthquake, the buildings most affected were schools, Coptic churches, and the Coptic Museum in old Cairo. In Cairo itself, 140 monuments were severely damaged, and—without preventive reinforcement—many remain today in danger of collapse.

Source: Natural Hazards (1994), 10: 261–74.

duction patterns, rendering old warehouses obsolete, and depriving historic cities of much of their technical, economic, and commercial basis. The cities and souks of Zabid and Old Shibam in Yemen, both on the World Heritage List, are eloquent examples of what are today dying monuments.

- *Agricultural expansion*, together with the expansion of irrigation systems and competition for land, results in encroachment on sites with important archaeological remains.

- *Air pollution* has emerged over recent decades as one of the gravest threats to old built structures. Industrialization has led to increased emissions of corrosive acidic pollutants such as sulfur oxides (Mourato 1997).

Social causes. Among the social causes of accelerated deterioration, the most typical are described below.

- *Population densities* have increased, mostly in urban settlements (e.g., in medinas of cultural value), accelerating the wear and tear on historic buildings. Demographic growth generates large amounts of solid and liquid waste, decreases maintenance, and triggers illegal construction and illegal demolition of the built heritage. High levels of rural-urban migration continue to increase densities in towns and coastal areas. For example, demographic projections indicate that Mediterranean coastal populations will grow from 82 million in 1990 to 150 million—170 million in 2025, sharpening competition for land and increasing pollution, among other effects.

- *Tourism*, which is intended to celebrate the historic patrimony and may contribute to saving it, can have destructive effects when it is commercialized beyond normal carrying capacities, bringing pollution, waste, and sometimes vandalism.

- *Looting, illegal excavations, and theft* from archaeological sites, repositories, and museums are among the most vicious forms of heritage destruction. "Grave robbers" are an old breed of enemies of the patrimony, but experts warn that the pace and scale of looting have greatly accelerated as a result of the use of modern techniques (such as explosives and powerful metal detectors that reveal caches of bronze, silver, and gold) and because of the "incentives" provided by unscrupulous dealers and by instant publicity about prices at international art auctions. By definition, most such destruction through looting goes unreported. When civil wars and political upheavals occur, controls break down completely, and vast areas become looting fields.

According to one international expert, "the destruction of heritage art in the last four decades represents a cultural disaster probably unmatched at any time in history, which has accelerated in the last ten years" (Melikian 1997).

- *Neglect and ignorance.* Last, but not least, lack of awareness of what is irreplaceable heritage and why it must be preserved also causes much loss. Many millions of people actually live in or use buildings that are part of the cultural patrimony, without being aware of it or of the sensitivity of the buildings to particular conditions. The result can be unwitting damage to the heritage (Amahan 1999). Education about the importance of CH is provided unevenly in MENA countries, and museums tend to play only a limited role in raising public awareness.

Weak governance—an aggravating factor. Natural, economic, and social factors coalesce in their corrosive action and amplify each other. The combined effects are highly detrimental to the built patrimony. For some assets, they are directly lethal, and these assets are lost forever. Unfortunately, such effects are aggravated by fully avoidable institutional weaknesses. Current patterns of governance over the patrimony are insufficient for coordinated, collective action by the social actors interested in safeguarding the heritage and are unable to stem the adverse natural, economic, and social impacts summarized above.

The need for reform. Improving the governance of the cultural patrimony is a task of national importance for every country. In sum, this analysis documents on a sectorwide basis the need to overcome weaknesses in institutional and organizational capacities (central and local) and in the updating of policy and legal frameworks. In developing longer-term strategies, the need to reform the current financing system for CH must be seen, in some countries, as including market-informed repricing of access fees and other services and better husbanding of the sector's own capacities for self-financing. Interlinked and coordinated master planning, rather than piecemeal action, is called for. The challenge is a

On the narrow stair-streets of Algiers' kasbah, house balconies and walls threatening to collapse are often supported by improvised exterior beams.

The construction of Egypt's huge Aswan Dam required the relocation of the Abu Simbel Temple and other monuments at a higher elevation, to a new, nearby site. A crane prudently lifts and relocates the statue of Ramses II.

Buried in the desert sands of eastern Syria, the Dura Europos Synagogue (built in 244 C.E.) was discovered after seventeen centuries, in 1932, with its frescoes still vivid: west wall panel with Aaron the high priest. Relocated and preserved now in the National Museum, Damascus.

national one, and it requires that the macrosectoral issues be addressed, to achieve many-sided improvements in the governance of the patrimony. The challenge is also international and calls for help from the international community, which has a stake in patrimony preservation. It is incumbent on the World Bank as well, as part of this international community, to examine critically its response to date and expand its contribution in the future.

The "conflict" preservation–development must be managed. The adverse impacts of infrastructure construction, agricultural expansion, and other factors—which are indispensable for MENA countries' development—point to a potential conflict between development objectives and patrimony conservation, in a way comparable to the development–environment dilemma or the development–population resettlement debate. This potential conflict should be neither exacerbated nor exaggerated. It is not unsolvable. It can be addressed through policies and special programs and can be effectively mitigated and limited. If the CH sector is to be incorporated into mainstream development policies and programs, it is incumbent on these programs to mount a credible and effective counteraction against the multiple causes of patrimony loss, including the causes embedded in the nature of development itself.

A national challenge. In sum, the contrast is stark between the luminous image of MENA's patrimony and the composite sectoral image of its losses through natural, economic, and social factors, combined with chronic weaknesses in institutional capacity and sectoral governance. This contrast sends an urgent call to the custodians of this heritage— MENA states, governments, and societies. Given the cultural pressures of globalization processes and the homogenizing impacts of imported cultural models, it is even more important today to reinforce the endurance of the national cultural heritage. The way to do this is to consider the overall sectoral situation, to recognize macrosector needs, and to address them at the level of policy, national institutional setups, and underlying economic and financial infrastructure. The management of the patrimony is emerging today as a growing issue on MENA countries' development agenda. It is a national challenge.

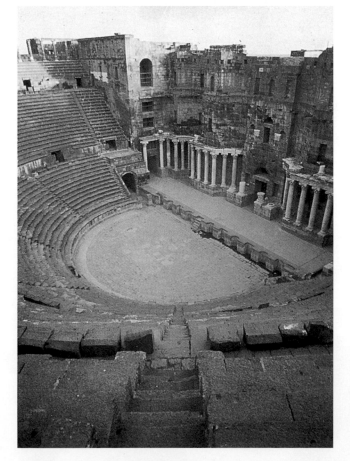

The grand Roman amphitheater of Bosra, Syria, regarded as the best-preserved Roman theater in existence, was built early in the 2nd century C.E., when Bosra became the capital of the new Roman province of Arabia.

Iran: The grand Shah Mosque of Isfahan (17th century) with its typical architectural vocabulary of domes, arches, minarets.

CHAPTER 2

Cultural Heritage and World Bank Policies

Given the major sectoral constraints described in the foregoing chapter, and the massive losses being incurred by MENA countries' patrimony, the obvious questions are: Can the World Bank help MENA countries overcome these constraints? Does Bank policy offer scope for addressing the complex CH needs confronted by MENA governments?

The evolution of World Bank policy on cultural heritage. The Bank's Board and management recently provided an important framework for action that synthesizes several Bank policies relevant to the general issues of culture in development and to the particular issues of preserving heritage (World Bank 1999a). These policies have evolved considerably over time. The Bank's policy statements dedicated specifically to cultural patrimony issues are in fact part of the Bank's policy stand about the cultural content of economic development and about the interaction between social, cultural, economic, and technological factors of development. This broader policy stand has been voiced increasingly, starting from the early 1980s, in various policy papers, occasional statements, and numerous publications.

The Bank's specific policies relevant to cultural patrimony were formulated starting from the early 1980s, in particular the policy on indigenous peoples living in areas of Bank-financed projects (issued in 1982 and expanded in 1997) and the policy on protecting cultural assets discovered by chance in areas of World Bank–funded projects (OPN 11.03, 1986).[10] More recent statements are contained also in Bank policy papers on poverty reduction, environmental protection, and social inclusion (Wolfensohn 1997) and in other documents. Because the Bank's policies relevant for the CH domain are not widely known, a summary of their content and evolution follows. Chapter III will in turn discuss the economic foundation of the Bank's policy and of its interventions for CH management.

"Do not harm the heritage." The 1986 operational policy OPN 11.03 expressed a strong "do not harm the heritage" posture. It made mandatory the protection of assets accidentally unearthed by civil works under Bank-financed projects. According to the policy, the Bank assists only those projects that are designed and sited so as to avoid, minimize, or mitigate adverse impacts on cultural property, and it will not finance projects that damage cultural heritage. If project works might endanger cultural property, the policy requires that staff and borrowers take action to (a) relocate project activities; (b) adjust the project design so that sites and structures can be conserved, studied, documented, and, as appropriate, preserved in situ; or (c) as a last resort, and jointly with national authorities, selectively relocate the cultural property to conserve, study, document, and restore it at an alternate site.

The Bank has tenaciously negotiated the implementation of this policy with borrowing agencies, opposing long-entrenched damaging practices. Results have fully validated the approach of OPN 11.03. For instance, in several MENA countries the policy succeeded in safeguarding important cultural assets accidentally discovered on project sites. (See Box 2.1 on a recent CH discovery in a West Bank–Gaza project.) The policy also helps increase public awareness about the need for regulated preservation of historic assets. This cultural policy remains in force and is regularly applied by the MENA region.

Limitations of the protection policy. When it was adopted, the "do not harm" stance was an advance over previous practices, which had been oblivious to the cultural heritage. Nonetheless, it only amounts to CH assistance by happenstance and piecemeal. Gradually, both the Bank and MENA governments have come to realize the limitations of this policy and the need for a more proactive position. The reasons are twofold:

- A "do not harm" approach is relatively passive and limited to chance; it does not bring cultural assets into the country's economic development circuit.

- Although this approach truly snatches some major "cultural finds" from the bulldozer's jaws, and rescues them for posterity, it remains silent vis-à-vis long-known (and often even more important) cultural assets that form the core of the national patrimony. When deprived of preservation resources, these core assets deteriorate silently and rapidly.

The 1999 framework for action. The framework for action on culture in development was endorsed by the Bank's Board of Executive Directors, together with a new work program. The MENA region's CH activities are reflected in this framework and work plan. The framework reempha-

---

BOX 2.1

The Byzantine Basilica at Jabalia

The discovery of the Byzantine Basilica at Jabalia, on the outskirts of Gaza City, occurred as a result of a major public works program funded in West Bank–Gaza under the first Bank-assisted Emergency Rehabilitation Project. The project is cofinanced by Saudi Arabia, Denmark, Kuwait, and Switzerland.

In the course of rebuilding Salah-El-Din Road at the gateway into Gaza, a backhoe operator struck toppled columns. Work was stopped immediately. On closer examination, the site proved to be a large basilica complex, comprising a church, baptistery and cemetery. It was constructed in the golden years of the Byzantine Empire, continued in use after the Islamic conquest, and is thought to have been abandoned only after being leveled by an earthquake in the eighth century C.E.

About 17 inscriptions that identify donors provide clues as to the history of the church. The site's great significance stems from the number of inscriptions found here, more than double the number in any other Byzantine church in the Mashreq countries of Syria, Lebanon, and Jordan. The oldest inscription dates to 444 C.E., during the reign of the Byzantine emperor Theodosius, and the latest inscription to 732 C.E., in the caliphate of Hisham Abdul Malik. The mosaics found in the Basilica are remarkable not only for their beauty and freshness but also as a mute testimony to past religious turmoil. (See the picture of a Jabalia mosaic on this publication's cover.)

Many discoveries were made under other projects. For example, a Canaanite fountain was discovered in the course of building an access road into Jenin under a Bank-financed project, and in another project, a sewer from the Hellenistic period, reportedly still in use, was found outside the Gaza municipal offices.

Source: Prepared by David Sewell.

---

sizes that all development interventions intrinsically involve cultural and social dimensions that must be understood and taken into account. Progress made by the Bank over the past two decades in incorporating cultural considerations into development interventions must continue. The key question for the Bank is no longer a conceptual one—whether culture matters—but a strategic and operational one: refining the means for making culture part of the purposive inducement of development, thus increasing the cultural sustainability of development and its economic effectiveness. The Bank supports both investment lending and nonlending assistance for improving heritage management in ways congruent with each country's priorities in development.

The 1999 framework for action opens up several new options:

- It *expands* the Bank's area of stated concern, from isolated "chance finds" to the core physical patrimony, with selectivity.

- It *asserts* the Bank's readiness to go beyond CH safeguard measures toward proactive capture of the patrimony's economic value, by financing high-impact CH projects based on newly defined criteria and avoiding CH projects with low or peripheral development impact.

- It *focuses* the Bank's CH work on the nexus between cultural heritage and development. In particular, it highlights the exploitable synergy between a proactive CH position and the Bank's central objectives of employment creation and poverty reduction.

These provisions broaden the range of options and instruments for assisting countries not only in discrete, location-specific CH preservation but also in addressing sectorwide development needs.

The famous ramparts with cannons of the town of Essaouira on Morocco's Mediterranian coast (bottom), are well preserved. But lack of resources leaves the city wall (top) crumbling and defenseless against erosion by sea and weather.

Consistent with the Bank's development rationale, the MENA region works to take into account sociocultural dimensions *throughout* its agenda. First, it does so at the level of every project intervention in agriculture, infrastructure, health, and other sectors.[11] Second, the MENA region has turned recently, more than in the past, to providing direct financial support

to high-impact projects focused on the cultural sector itself or to cultural heritage project components within urban sector projects, postconflict reconstruction projects, and tourism projects.

Bank policy and the patrimony's economic value. The Bank's policy toward CH rests on two cornerstones: the patrimony's economic value and its educational value.

By definition, the patrimony represents a vast collection of *cultural* assets, but these assets also have a huge *economic* value. Markets only imperfectly recognize this economic value because of insufficient information and inadequate pricing mechanisms. Historically, the economic value of the patrimony's endowments has been given much less attention than its cultural significance. Largely because of this limited recognition, policymakers and planners in developing countries have been little concerned, and little able, to activate and harvest the economic value of their countries' patrimony. Bank policy has come to unambiguously recognize this economic value. It holds that the patrimony can become an auxiliary engine for generating economic growth and development.

Poverty reduction. The orientation toward poverty alleviation is one of the new and distinct policy perspectives that the Bank brings to bear on the CH domain, compared with agencies that have as their primary purpose technical conservation work, artistic restoration, or heritage research. Since its overarching mandate is poverty reduction, the Bank's assistance to CH management aims to find ways to channel, to the extent possible, the patrimony's economic benefits toward employment creation and poverty reduction. This orientation is deeply convergent with the basic needs of MENA countries. It is also conducive to new forms of CH assistance. Poverty-related impacts result when investments in CH diversify income generation, create new jobs, and improve the living standards of poor communities and neighborhoods, primarily around heritage sites. The economic reasons for Bank support to CH are further discussed in detail in Chapter III.

The educational value of the patrimony. The second cornerstone of the Bank's CH policy is the emphatic recognition that the patrimony has intrinsic noneconomic—spiritual, moral, and political—value; in short, it has enormous educational value. These noneconomic values are in themselves a solid argument for investment in preservation of the patrimony, economic benefits aside. Cultural patrimony assets are not just "commodities." Their educational capability is unsubstitutable. The patrimony is essential for human capital formation and for inculcating national identity. Material cultural objects help "objectify" and assert identity. The patrimony contributes to fostering human bonds inside and across borders and to forming social capital. For national governments, these attributes fully justify financial investments on strictly cultural grounds, as well.

Globalization and heritage. The educational value of the cultural heritage becomes even more relevant in light of the currently expanding trends toward globalization. Heritage awareness is not innate; it requires targeted education. If good management is indispensable for harvesting the patrimony's economic value, awareness raising is similarly indispensable for realizing its educational capabilities. Heritage preservation is more than glorifying physical objects; it entails acquiring meanings about history and identity. Collectivities lose their grasp on their communal and cultural traditions at their own peril. Cultural heritage is the collective memory of nations. Without it, there can be no answer to the perennial questions human groups ask about themselves: Who were we? Who are we? Who are we going to become? Contemporary trends toward globalization only make the cultural answers to these questions more important to each nation.

Although economic globalization trends sometimes increase cultural diversity, more often they tend to pose a risk to cultural pluralism, increase uniformity, and cause loss of diversity. In resisting the homogenizing trends entailed by globalization of trade and communication, cultural identity and diversity can be reinforced and safeguarded through preservation of patrimony. "If we all are to build a good global village, we need first to know well the village we are coming from" (Sarbib 2000). Stronger cultural identities can in turn enable societies to participate, with greater contributions, in the positive effects of globalization trends and communication exchanges, while fending off culturally standardizing influences. From this perspective, the incorporation of heritage management into development strategies appears just as beneficial on educational grounds as on economic grounds.

The question of the Bank's comparative advantage in the CH sector. Taking a proactive investment stance in the patrimony sector raises a legitimate question that the Bank has faced in the past as well, whenever it has become involved in new domains such as the environment, health care, and education. Does the Bank have a specific comparative advantage for assisting this domain? If yes, what is it? If not, why should the Bank get involved?

The issue of comparative advantage has caused some controversy and has elicited polarized responses, some exaggerating the value added by the Bank, others denying it. The discussion is not completely closed, but practice increasingly offers testimony about the specific kind of Bank value-adding contributions. These are two-fold: value-adding contributions to overall development effectiveness in related sectors and value-adding to the CH sector itself.

A major practical advantage of the Bank is its ability to help incorporate impactful CH assistance into mainstream development programming as a development partner to governments not just in one or another sector but for entire economies. The patrimony stands to gain more from numerous integrated projects in multiple sectors of the economy. This opens up opportunities for CH support through a multitude of Bank sectoral investments—for instance, in infrastructure, urban development, education, tourism, and agriculture.

More value added can result from enlisting CH investments in the service of the core poverty reduction and employment objectives. Factual examination in the course of this review has shown that ongoing CH components have been tailored to converge with poverty reduction goals. Evidence of actual impacts is expected from completed project evaluation studies.

The economic prosperity of the village of Sidi Bou Said, Tunisia, largely depends on the many shops selling delicately colored pottery and countless other handicraft items.

Comparative advantage is further manifest in the Bank's ability, for instance, to (a) support CH institutional capacity building as part of national institutional reforms, improving management patterns in the CH area; (b) help reform the sector's financing and self-financing arrangements; and (c) support national strategy and programming for the CH sector at large, in coordination with national development strategies and goals. As this analysis shows (see also Chapter IV), ongoing projects in Jordan and Morocco are already building on this comparative advantage.

Government views on the World Bank's comparative advantage. During the consultations undertaken for this study, the comparative advantage issues were examined by asking governments whether, from their perspective, the Bank has or lacks a comparative advantage in CH assistance. According to government officials in several MENA countries, the international assistance for CH received by these countries in recent years, which is widely perceived as insufficient, has not been integrated cross-sectorally in the way outlined above. Jordan's minister of culture, for instance, has stated that "there is a clear deficiency in supporting culture in our country, whether at the national or international level. . . . Most international loans are stipulated to certain fields, but the last is the culture field" (Al-Rfou'h 1999). Increased support, combined with better integration into broader national development strategies, can successfully tap latent cross-sectoral synergies and maximize benefits not just for CH preservation but also for the overall economy.

The government officials consulted regard the patrimony as their country's "national comparative advantage"—an advantage that can be better realized if it "meshes with" the Bank's comparative advantage and its ability to help the patrimony bear more development fruit. Systematic cross-sectoral integration of CH support is increasingly perceived as more likely to yield added benefits to the country, on a wider scale, than can "insular," piecemeal interventions.

Operational implications. From these comparative advantage considerations, two key operational principles emerge for the MENA region: selectivity and partnership building.

- *Selectivity.* The selectivity principle, at the country or state level, guides MENA to choose and support CH activities that are germane to the Bank's core mandate and are apt to yield large development benefits. Neither the importance nor the ubiquity of worthy heritage sites guarantees that every preservation intervention is necessarily a priority and will have high development impacts. It is hence imperative to weigh alternative project options and avoid those with peripheral impacts; leverage the Bank's comparative advantages; understand not only what the Bank could do, but also what it should not do in the cultural sector or where it does not have a comparative advantage; and most important, embed heritage protection *within*, rather than parallel to, the Bank's development strategies of poverty reduction, infrastructure financing, and social inclusion. Bank intervention in the CH domain should not crowd out the private sector or other agencies. The Bank will explicitly step back where other institutions have a clear comparative advantage, and it will not invest when alternative financing is available. Selectivity will be implemented through the use of discerning criteria for granting or declining Bank lending (see Chapter V).

- *Partnerships.* Awareness of its comparative advantages and disadvantages leads the Bank to build partnerships. One of the current comparative disadvantages is that the number of staff members in MENA with the skills required for CH activities is still limited. Inviting the expertise of specialized organizations is therefore paramount, together with building up MENA's in-house skills. "Much of the knowledge on the various aspects of culture, . . ." stated the Bank's president, "resides outside of the World Bank. Therefore, integrating culture into the Bank's work will depend on successful partnerships. Partnerships that bring together international, regional, national, and local actors; that bridge formal and informal, private and public sectors. Partnerships that bring in foundations, civil society, and the communities themselves, as well as national governments and international agencies" (Wolfensohn 1999a).

Key partner institutions. The Bank and its MENA region have pursued, and will continue to implement, a firm course of partnership with UNESCO, in particular. Within the UN system, the World Bank's lending for culture is informed by the normative frameworks and the technical analyses and recommendations of UNESCO, which has been working in this domain for about half a century and has vast expertise not present in the Bank. The MENA region also promotes cooperation with regional and international cultural NGOs such as ICOMOS, ICCROM, ICOM, the Aga Khan Trust for Culture (AKTC), the Center for Jewish Art (CJA), and others; with other multilateral donors (for example, UNDP, the Arab Fund, the European Union, the Organisation for Economic Co-operation and Development, and various international foundations), with the bilateral aid agencies of industrial countries, and so on.[12] There is much that the Bank as an institution and its staff have to learn from these organizations.

Partnerships as a two-way street. While inviting new partners, MENA in turn is prepared to help specialized cultural agencies that seek certain capacities from the Bank to reinforce their own work. The MENA region's convening ability and influence with governments and the private sector can empower other agencies' work and help place CH issues on the main development track. Complementarities through partnerships reinforce all partners.

Cross-sectoral links and CH institution building. Consistent with its comparative advantage, the Bank promotes cross-sectoral approaches and institutional mechanisms for interministerial cooperation. This policy orientation is highly relevant for the cultural sector in MENA countries. The analysis reported in this paper shows that, despite differences of degree from country to country, weak institutional capacity for CH management is a widespread characteristic. It is crucial to overcome the gaps and the absence of partnering relations among the central ministries (culture, finance, tourism, infrastructure, artisanat, environment, etc.) whose activities relate to the country's patrimony. Another avenue for multiplying capacity is involvement of regional and municipal authorities, rather than exclusive central authority over the patrimony. The promotion of cross-sectoral links and of interministerial synergies, replacing insular institutional approaches, is a CH policy cornerstone for the Bank.

Traditional silver jewelry of Yemen.

Egypt: Tall and slender minarets, old and new, dominate the Cairo skyline

CHAPTER 3

Economic Benefits and Poverty Reduction Through CH Preservation

This chapter addresses the economic aspects of CH support interventions. Sound development policy requires that investment decisions and economic assistance to CH rely on robust economic analysis, and the Bank approach promotes and requires such analysis. Patrimony assets already play a role in the overall economy of the MENA region. It is a matter of good policy to base further investment decisions in the patrimony on a clear economic rationale.

The basic economic questions asked about providing Bank assistance to the patrimony sector are similar, in essence, to those for other sectors, with due adjustments for the cultural nature of assets. What are the relations between costs and benefits? Are the opportunity costs of using scarce resources for the CH sector, rather than for other demands, justified? What valuation techniques are available for assessing the economic value of patrimony endowments? What kinds of economic and noneconomic impacts for the society at large can be reasonably expected from such investments? If investments above current levels are made, will the incremental benefits justify the incremental expenditures?

Furthermore, given that the policy focus of the Bank's assistance is poverty alleviation, it is important to examine whether investments in CH and the gains from them can be so channeled as to contribute to reducing poverty and creating jobs for people condemned to poverty because of unemployment.

To some, such questions about economic payoffs may seem narrow-minded when they refer to preserving culture. But they are not, because investment resources are scarce, and responsible economic analysis is indispensable. Willingly or unwillingly, in everyday practice the survival of cultural assets is deeply influenced by economic criteria. Opportunity cost considerations, for instance, regularly intervene in decisionmaking by public administrators on whether to approve or decline one or another preservation investment (see Fey 1997; Throsby 1997). Therefore, it is indeed necessary to improve economic methodologies and the overall economic rationale of support for the CH domain. Moreover, if investing in CH management can pass the test of economic analysis, much of the current hesitation vis-à-vis such investments could be overcome.

Public goods: the national dimension. The fundamental rationale for using public resources in CH preservation agencies is grounded in the well-known economic theory of public goods. There is much similarity between cultural goods and environmental goods (or biodiversity). Cultural patrimony assets are public goods. They provide benefits that are nonrival and nonexcludable. As public goods, they can be enjoyed by all, without any one person's "consumption" and enjoyment diminishing or preventing the enjoyment of others.[13] As a body of goods, they provide unsubstitutable cultural and economic services. The benefits they generate are both intra- and intergenerational.

Because heritage assets are public goods, they need—and justify— public expenditures for their upkeep and for maintaining their ability to satisfy specific needs of present and future generations. It is generally recognized that markets do not function efficiently in setting at optimal levels and capturing the use-value of patrimony goods and services. The general interest requires public sector intervention to correct such market inefficiencies, while ensuring access and benefits for all potential users. Because the social "wants" related to patrimony use cannot be satisfied, or fully satisfied, through market processes only, they must be provided for by complementing the market with state intervention through budget mechanisms. This is why governments have the lead role in making various CH public goods accessible to their citizens and to humanity at large, in both present and future generations.

Public goods: the global dimension. The case for public financial support to patrimony assets as public goods is currently being strengthened by the expanding debate about the global nature of certain public goods—environmental or cultural—and about the definition of global public goods. Not all cultural patrimony assets have universal significance, but some indisputably do—for example, those already on UNESCO's World Heritage List, many of them located in MENA countries (see location maps at end of study). Their benefits are transnational. People from all over the world travel to MENA countries to share in the knowledge and emotions of seeing and learning from these cultural treasures of universal relevance. Cultural diversity is a global public good, like biodiversity, and maintaining it requires public support. Investments that maintain and enhance global public goods will generate additional national and transnational benefits.

The universal value of some patrimony public goods located in developing countries justifies and demands international aid for their maintenance and more development cooperation in the CH sector. New forms of international financial assistance to developing countries are required to support the preservation, sustainable "supply," and management of these fragile and endangered global cultural public goods, from which humankind benefits. Although all these implications are not discussed here, it is nonetheless important to point to the expanding international discussion on global public goods and the evolving new concepts (Kaul, Grunberg, and Stern 1999).

Economic value. While the theory of public goods legitimizes public intervention for CH support, it does not, and cannot, answer specific questions regarding amounts, valuation methods, costs, and benefits. Yet these questions are faced in practice every time when decisions on conservation and management are made. The answers depend on the economic valuation of cultural endowments and on the methods used for measuring and capturing their economic value. Although the discipline of cultural economics is only at its beginning, and many issues are being researched, knowledge is emerging from experience and can increasingly inform decisionmaking (Pearce forthcoming).[14] In recent years, economic research has begun to yield analytical and evaluative evidence, and work in the new field of cultural economics is expanding (Pagiola 1996).[15] The World Bank's Development Economics vice presidency has started its own program of research on culture, cultural heritage, and development (Alkire, Rao, and Woolcock 1999).[16] Many of the economic analytical techniques needed for intervention in the CH area are being adapted from environmental economics, which a decade or two ago faced the same new demand to apply economic analysis to investment in environmental protection.

There is broad agreement to date on several economic propositions:

- Cultural assets, like environmental goods, have economic value.

- These economic values and potentials can increasingly be assessed through improved methodologies, as discussed below.

- Most important, their economic value can be captured, and even maximized, through adequate policies and efficient pricing.

These propositions reinforce the argument of the public goods theory.

Difficulties do emerge, however, in practical economic evaluations because of limited experience and insufficient research. Policymakers have to weigh the opportunity costs of investing in CH compared to alternative investments. Resource scarcity and competing needs complicate such decisions. "If cultural assets attracted extremely high economic values, or if intrinsic values always prevailed, then cultural heritage could not be under threat. The fact that it is threatened suggests that its economic value is either low or is not realized. Research suggests that the latter is often the case: there is a substantial economic value, but it is not 'captured' by those who either own the assets or who have the duty to conserve them" (Pearce and Mourato forthcoming). The road to harvesting these unrealized values must therefore go through the economic valuation of cultural assets.

Valuation of cultural assets. Two aspects need to be considered in the economic valuation of CH assets: identification of value, and measurement of value. It is widely recognized that conventional yardsticks are hardly usable in this domain. Instead, economic analysis has identified several types of use and nonuse economic values of cultural assets that are generally accepted and can be taken into account in investment decisionmaking. They are:

- *Direct use values:* those directly related to the actual use of cultural goods, such as visits to and adaptation and reuse of historic buildings

- *Indirect use values:* those related to benefits derived indirectly from patrimony goods, such as induced business opportunities, employment in services, and so on

- *Option values:* those derived from the individual's (or the group's) desire to retain the option to benefit from the asset some time in the future

- *Bequest values, or nonuse values:* those resulting from people's intention to bequeath the assets to future generations

- *Existence values:* those related to people's desire to know that heritage sites exist and are maintained, even though they themselves may never enjoy them.

Economists have devised several ways of measuring the values of heritage assets, even though such measurements are difficult (since significant cultural values will arise outside the market). These alternative means of measurement are defined as contingent valuation methods (CVMs), whereby people's willingness to pay for the use of the asset (or willingness to accept compensation for its loss) is estimated through surveys of potential beneficiaries. Contingent valuation depends on the meanings and worth attributed by people to certain assets or sites (Throsby 1997).[17] These measurement methods are obviously not perfect and are subject to continuous refinement, But they represent the improving economic state of the art,

equip public administrators with a framework for economic decisionmaking, and
help them actualize the economic potential
of assets and recover the costs of their protection.[18]

**Heritage management: a "value-add-
ing" industry.** The economically "cap-
turable" values of cultural assets depend on
the worth people tend to assign to them.
Good heritage management can enhance
these values and make them easier to harvest, while safeguarding the assets effec-

tively. Far from being just a liability to national budgets, as some one-
sidedly regard it, the patrimony is—and can increasingly become—
a "value-adding" industry. "Heritage management adds value to existing
assets that have either ceased to be viable or that never were economically productive because their location area is too hot, or too cold, or too
wet, or too dry, or too remote, or because they are operated outside the
realm of profit. . . . Heritage organizations ensure that places and practices in danger of disappearing because they are no longer occupied, or
functioning, or valued . . . will survive" (Kirshenblatt-Gimblett 1998: 150).

The economic opportunity to enhance further this value added
emerges from the complementarity between "preservation" and "management." Preservation is an essential premise of good CH management,
but management adds value to and builds on preservation, making the
preserved assets more accessible to larger numbers of people. This is why
heritage management and the tourism industry must collaborate. This is
also why the Bank's comparative advantage results from its ability not just
to finance preservation but also to integrate the management of CH into
the overall *management* of development.

The range of economic and noneconomic high impacts. Improved
management of patrimony assets can yield a spectrum of multiple, distinct, and incremental benefits. Broadly, these can be divided into economic and noneconomic high impacts, as follows:

Economic impacts
- Positive impacts on poverty reduction
- Positive impacts on national employment levels
- Positive impacts on total outputs and revenue levels from cultural
  industries and service industries
- Positive impacts on foreign exchange earnings.

Noneconomic impacts

- Beneficial impacts on educational levels and identity cultivation
- Beneficial impacts on social cohesion, inclusion and social capital development
- Beneficial impacts on continuously enlarging the nations' cultural patrimony
- Beneficial impacts on safeguarding and sustainably conveying the heritage to future generations.

Both sets of impacts or benefits are tremendously important. Ways of harvesting them through development intervention are outlined in detail in Chapter V and are documented extensively in the full-length regional sector study.

Targeting benefits from CH. Consistent with the Bank's economic and social rationale, it is important not only to capture and increase these benefits but also to channel them toward the nation's development priorities and needs. With respect to channeling and distributing the benefits from CH, Bank economic analysis is primarily concerned with (a) poverty reduction and the possible contribution of the CH sector, (b) potential for employment creation through tourism intermediation and beyond, and (c) the choices available to MENA governments when they weigh resource scarcity for investments in the patrimony. These aspects will be examined in turn.

Can CH contribute to poverty reduction? Since its overarching mandate is poverty reduction, the Bank's assistance to CH attempts to find ways to channel, to the extent possible, the patrimony's economic benefits toward poverty reduction objectives. Poverty-related impacts result when investments in CH diversify income generation, create new jobs, and improve the living standards of the poor, who often reside near heritage sites and sometimes even within heritage areas. The orientation toward poverty alleviation, as one of the distinct policy perspectives that the Bank brings to bear on the CH domain, calls for targeted attention to poor neighborhoods in or near CH sites and to assistance to community-driven projects for heritage management.

The geography of poverty. It is sometimes asked whether the orientation toward poverty reduction is not incongruous with patrimony preservation and is not artificially forced on it by the "development perspective." Realities on the ground provide the answer. The typical geography of poverty in MENA countries shows that most historic medinas (Fès, Algiers, Tunis, Kairouan, Tyr, Shibam, Aleppo, Damascus, Meknes, and others) contain large urban poor populations living in the midst of areas of former historic splendor. In Fès, the Bank's socioeconomic survey found that the poverty incidence among the medina populations is much higher than the average urban poverty rate for the entire country—a huge 36 percent, compared with 7.6 percent nationwide. Out of the population of 150,000 people, over 52,000 live below the defined poverty threshold (Navez 1995; Tagemouati 2000). In Fès-j'did the proportion of the poor population was higher: 48 percent. Urban overcrowding, crumbling infrastructure, decaying buildings, and poor sanitation condemn many medina inhabitants to low living standards and prevent the incubation of new businesses. This situation eliminates sizable quarters from tourism circuits and diminishes the chances for economic revitalization. Many rural areas, often rich in historic monuments, are also pockets of entrenched poverty. Thus, the very geography of poverty calls for convergence between heritage management support and poverty reduction efforts.

Creation of new employment. The case for activating the patrimony's latent economic value also relies on inducing incremental employment. MENA countries face many common critical problems. "Perhaps the greatest single issue facing the economies of the Middle East and North Africa is the challenge of employing its people . . . The problem of job creation in the MENA region is staggering" (van Eeghen and Keller

The old dance of the whirling dervish is kept alive by professional performers in Syria, as well as by religious adherents throughout the region.

1999). Unemployment rates are well above 10 percent in virtually every country in the region, and between 1999 and 2003 there will be about 17 million new entrants into the labor force. The search for additional ways to expand employment compels attention to CH opportunities as well. It is estimated, for instance, that the Fès-Medina project will create about 10,000 new jobs and additional small businesses (World Bank 1999b).

Employment gains through tourism intermediation. Massive economic benefits attributable to the existence of the patrimony accrue through the intermediation of tourism, international and domestic. Within the tourism sector, the domain in which most MENA countries hold comparative advantage is cultural tourism. Expanding it depends largely on investments in CH safeguarding and management. Morocco, for instance, derives about 7 percent of its GDP from the general (including cultural) tourism sector. The amount of foreign currency from tourism is the second most

important item after remittances from Moroccans working abroad. Yet the share of tourism in Morocco's GDP is about 50 percent lower than the global average and about 2.4 times smaller than the share of tourism in Greece's GDP. Morocco aims at doubling the number of incoming tourists, from 2 million just before year 2000 to about 4 million by 2010. According to some specialists' estimates, the number can be as much as quadrupled, with priority emphasis on showcasing the cultural patrimony.[19] Yet this cannot be accomplished without increased investment in improving CH management. (See the discussion in endnote 28.)

Direct employment occurs inside and outside the sites as a result of expenditures for site preservation and returns from the use of site and support facilities, linking cultural services with related services. In England, for instance, studies have confirmed the effectiveness of using cultural sites as poles of attraction in a "policy for depressed regions" and "in areas of high unemployment" (Johnson and Thomas 1990). In Tunisia the initial employment created per hotel bed from construction totals 2.8 person-years, to which is added recurrent employment of between 1.37 and 1.80 person-years annually per hotel bed, depending on hotel occupancy rates (see Box 3.1). These are averages for general tourism; growing, although not yet definitive, evidence suggests that expenditures by cultural tourists are higher than those by beach tourists.

To conclude, the evidence—still sporadic, but increasing as more research is done—suggests that employment in the CH sector and in related cultural tourism services is an impactful major avenue for absorbing a significant segment of the unemployed. Direct services to tourists and handicraft production and sale are labor-intensive activities. Governments in the region generally accept employment generation as an explicit reason for and objective of public funding for tourism stimulation programs. What is not consistently taken into account is that, ultimately, one major component of general tourism—that is, cultural tourism—directly depends on the condition of the CH sites.

These types of employment impacts can be channeled primarily, although not exclusively, toward geographic poverty pockets and the poor. Operational modalities for such channeling are numerous. Using them with priority depends both on targeted policies and on skilled craftsmanship in project selection and design. It is precisely this kind of focused investment in CH management that can derive increased benefits both for safeguarding the patrimony for the future and for immediate poverty reduction in the present.

Opportunity costs and resource scarcity issues. Opportunity costs are important in decisions to allocate resources for CH. Countries facing many competing demands for the same scarce financial resources hardly

---

BOX 3.1

Creation of New Employment by Hotel Bed in Tunisia

An economic survey in Tunisia breaks down the incremental person-years of employment per hotel bed per year into three domains: construction, services, and indirect activities.

- **Construction. *Investments*** in the construction of tourism hotels and other tourism-related infrastructure total 2.8 person-years per hotel bed. Of this amount, 1.3 person-years per hotel bed are accounted for by the construction industries proper; this figure consists of 0.9 person-year from the initial investment; 0.1 person-year from renovations; and 0.3 person-year from other infrastructure. In other infrastructure industries related to hotel construction, the total is 1.5 person-years per hotel bed.

- ***Services.*** Direct employment in services for the use of one hotel bed per year is 0.88 person-year at a hotel occupancy rate of 40 percent and 1.12 person-years at an occupancy rate of 56 percent.

- ***Indirect activities.*** Indirect employment created in agriculture and other indirect activities per hotel bed per year comes to 0.59 person-year at a hotel occupancy rate of 40 percent and 0.78 person-year at an occupancy rate of 56 percent.

Employment gains in construction occur in one round. Gains in services and indirect activities are recurrent and may increase each year when occupancy rates go higher than 40 or 56 percent. They may also decrease or increase with lower or higher amounts of expenditures per tourist. The trend in international tourism has been and continues to be toward significant increases in expenditure per tourist, leading to more employment per tourist or per hotel bed.

Source: Mitchell and Tunisian National Tourist Office (1995).

---

have "free resources" to shift toward the patrimony. This is why, usually, scarcity of budgetary resources and opportunity costs are the arguments invoked against state investment in CH management. This argument holds that the resources needed by the patrimony sector could be used for alternative investments that would also bear on development and poverty reduction, with similar or better results. This reasoning must be taken seriously, as it stems from a painful awareness of resource scarcity even for innovative approaches.

Indeed, alternative uses are always possible. Prudent management must weigh alternatives and their likely returns. But emerging economic assessments document that many CH investments can hold their own in terms of overall returns and impacts when compared with competing demands for limited resources.

A trader sells spices and fruits in a caravansery of the souk of Sana'a, Yemen. The souk remains to date a very powerful and diversified economic, artisanal, and cultural center.

In Sana'a's silver souk, Yahia Rassam restores and sells old Yemeni silver filigree jewelry. Periodically, he also takes his rare stock of precious wares to international fairs in Germany and Italy.

Four arguments in the scarcity-investment discussion. The following four reasons show why, even under conditions of budgetary scarcity, alternative investments do not necessarily outbid the patrimony off the investment agenda.

First, the key economic reason for the cultural patrimony case is that a vast body of valuable assets, for which sunk costs have already been paid by prior generations, is available. It is a waste to overlook such assets, yet much of the existing patrimony is insufficiently activated and lies dormant. Potential gains are forgone. A high opportunity cost is paid by not using the patrimony's potential, and this cost must be accounted for in alternative investments. A broad consensus has emerged that, despite recent progress, the economic value of the patrimony remains significantly underused. Without the clear-sighted will to make the necessary seed investments, the patrimony will underproduce and will further lose value through deterioration.

Second, beyond the strictly economic dimension, states have a major national interest in preserving the patrimony for future generations, and this too must be factored in when scarcity influences decisions. The reasoning in the CH case is comparable, mutatis mutandis, with the reasoning for a national interest in investing in security or in a clean environment, where the opportunity cost considerations of making or not making the requisite expenditures also intervene.

Third, knowledge about capturing the potential of the patrimony is only incipient. Learning how to do it must be facilitated through prudent investments rather than preempted by denying the needed seed resources for piloting. Macroeconomic research in the United States has shown that benefits from CH can significantly exceed benefits from some other industries, including manufacturing (see Box 3.2, below). If this holds true, opportunity costs appear in a different light and may be offset by higher gains. Developing countries need to invest in experimenting with and learning innovative ways of using the patrimony's endowments and thus derive new types and levels of benefits that are still unsuspected and untapped.

Fourth, the opportunity costs/scarcity argument tends to overlook the additionality of the vast range of noneconomic and economic benefits. Although some of the immediate benefits of CH sites do not enter markets, they are nonetheless benefits, real and incremental. The educational, moral, cultural, and political benefits from CH are the kind of immediate public benefit that cannot be purchased by any alternative investment. They are of great importance for the larger purposes of development, even if they cannot be subjected to monetary measurement. The limitations of economic measurements should not be imputed to the intrinsic or derived value of culture.

Who decides? How are scarcity-constrained investment choices to be made? Governments and civil societies alike in Maghreb and Mashreq countries express increasing concern about safely preserving their cultural patrimony and aim to correct the very insufficient participation of this sector in national growth-enhancing strategies. It is this realization that has already triggered several government requests to the Bank for project assistance to the CH sector. Given the need to manage scarcity and consider opportunity costs at the country level, it remains a point of regionwide policy for MENA, as well as for the Bank at large, that how much or how little a country will invest in CH preservation is to be determined by each country and society. Notwithstanding its readiness to provide financial assistance when justified, the MENA region emphasizes in its policy dialogue with governments that scarcity of resources is an important issue which should be recognized, not underestimated. Decisions should be based on country assessment of needs, priorities, and desired impacts and should be made with broad public awareness and involvement. The Bank carefully considers ways to address scarcity when it defines its country assistance strategies (CASs) and includes in them support for CH based on impact-maximization reasoning.

Pursuing impact multipliers. Given existing scarcities, investments in heritage management have a higher justification when they become impact multipliers; that is, when they generate cascading economic and noneconomic benefits—primary, secondary, and tertiary—with a direct bearing on reducing poverty within and around the heritage sites and on creating new jobs even far away from the heritage sites proper.

Policy solutions for overcoming scarcity. Scarcity must be pragmatically addressed in other ways than by taking the line of least resistance and ranking CH lowest on the investment totem pole, with the smallest allocation. The policy alternative is to amplify the supply of financial resources from alternative sources. The Bank's stance is that public funds, including Bank-supplied funds, should not be regarded as the sole source for CH. More stakeholders than the state alone, both domestic and international, are interested in preservation, and all have the responsibility and incentives to contribute financially.

BOX 3.2

Economic Benefits of Historic Building Rehabilitation for Re-use

An econometric model developed by the Bureau of Economic Analysis of the U.S. Department of Commerce measures the local impact of output from a variety of economic activities. 528 types of activities were evaluated and then consolidated into 39 industry groups. As performance indicators, the following three input-output multipliers were used to quantify the impact of production in the 39 groups: number of jobs created, increase in household income, and total impact on the rest of the economy.

The data were compiled by state. The table reflects present-value data for the state of California, and the "relationship between variables would be similar throughout the United States." Since it is often assumed that manufacturing activities have the greatest economic impact, the comparison in the table is between rehabilitation of buildings and the average of the 17 principal manufacturing categories in the 39 groups.

Input-Output Multipliers in U.S. Industries

Indicator	Benefits from U.S.$1 million invested in:	
	Manufacturing industries	Building rehabilitation
Additional jobs (number of jobs)	21.3	31.3
Additional household income (U.S. dollars)	553,700	833,500
Value added to the economy's output (U.S. dollars)	1,109,665	1,402,800

Source: Rypkema (1998).

The column for manufacturing industries in the table gives an average for 17 industry groups. The researchers thought that it was legitimate to ask how many of these 17 industries, taken individually, have higher multipliers than building rehabilitation. The answer was: none. Using the same unit of investment, not one of these 17 manufacturing sectors was found to exceed the input-output multipliers of the building rehabilitation for re-use.

The Bank's policy (a) calls for the coparticipation of the private business sector in CH assistance, (b) encourages voluntary contributions in various forms by civil society, and (c) requires Bank staff to actively assist governments in mobilizing grant aid cofinancing from other bilateral and international donors. Because of the patrimony's universal cultural value, and with World Bank support, seed domestic investments can be leveraged (often more easily than with investments in other sectors) into "magnets" for attracting other donors' grant aid, as well as for stimulating the customary local *mécénat* and various endowment factors.

Self-financing. The scarcity of resources can also be alleviated through policy and institutional reform for increasing the sector's self-financing. Best practices show that incremental self-financing can be attained in MENA countries through more efficient pricing of assets and services, differential visitor charges that maximize net revenue, changes in tax laws, new incentive levers, and more systematic involvement of local communities. Given supportive policy environments, the patrimony's own capacity for pivotal self-financing is just now beginning to be imaginatively explored.

Quantifying economic benefits. Going beyond the analysis of the MENA region proper, this review also researched the economic evidence available in other countries on the actual benefits from historic preservation. Such analyses, which have been carried out more often in industrial than in developing countries, have produced relevant findings. A recent econometric study in the United States compared returns to investments in historic building rehabilitation and reuse with investment returns in 17 manufacturing industries, along three indicators of input-output multipliers (see Box 3.2). The study concluded that "in all three categories—job creation, household income, and total impact—building rehabilitation consistently outperforms the manufacturing sector" (Rypkema 1998). In developing countries as well, studies have found that preservation with the re-use of old building for new functions practices can reduce investments and increase benefits and employment (Tagemouati 1999)

The same macroeconomic study identified seven different ways in which cultural historic preservation acts as a powerful "economic generator." These are (1) employment creation, (2) stimulation of heritage tourism, (3) small business incubation, (4) revitalization of the downtown in large cities, (5) economic revitalization of small towns, (6) neighbor-

Re-use of traditional buildings gives them new life and new functions while preserving culture and architecture in economically highly beneficial ways. The Dar El Jeld Restaurant in the kasbah of Tunis beneficially re-uses a rehabilitated classic Tunisian building.

hood stabilization, and (7) neighborhood diversity. Some of these routes may work less effectively in developing country contexts, but others, and particularly the first three, are likely to have stronger impacts in developing economies than in advanced industrial economies such as the United States.

Capturing heritage benefits at the project level. Is it possible to capture the economic values of patrimony assets using investment projects as development vehicles? The answer to this question is given by economic and financial analysis at the project level. The Morocco Fès-Medina Rehabilitation project, for instance, applied a full battery of economic analytical techniques, both conventional and novel, for assessing benefits (see Box 3.3). Each analysis consistently found an economic rate of return (ERR) of around 17 percent or more. When the Fès project estimated the use and nonuse values of the heritage with contingent valuation techniques, beyond the traditional cost-benefit analysis, the economic benefits appeared considerably higher. Project implementation will provide additional data. The methodology of project economic analysis for this category of investment is being further refined from one project to another.

Conclusion. To sum up, the economic rationale for supporting CH management is based on the public goods nature of CH assets and on their intrinsic capacity to produce high economic impacts. The economic values are identifiable, and the methodology of measuring them is continuously improving. Resource scarcity considerations are real,

Shibam, a World Heritage walled city in Yemen, is unique with its old mud-brick "skyscraper" buildings of 8, 9, or 10 floors. Public funds for maintaining such monuments are scarce or totally lacking. A private owner has started self-financed rehabilitation work, employing master builders skilled in traditional mud architecture.

however, and investment choices need to be made with careful consideration of opportunity costs both ways—that is, with and without allocations to patrimony management. Experience demonstrates that with good project design and improved management, economic values can be captured and benefits in this sector can be significantly increased (Pearce and Mourato forthcoming). Under Bank assistance approaches, benefits can be channeled in ways that will maximize their contribution to the basic development objectives of MENA countries, such as poverty reduction and employment creation. Noneconomic benefits, particularly in education, nation building, and identity cultivation, are also major. Taken together, these elements provide a realistic and sound economic rationale for domestic CH policies and interventions.

BOX 3.3

Economic Analyses in the Fès-Medina Project

The number of economic analytical tests to which the investments in the Fès-Medina project were subjected significantly exceeded the usual level of project economic analysis.

- First, an initial cost-benefit analysis was done on investments for improved medina access, resulting in an economic rate of return (ERR) of 17 percent. A related economic analysis was done on congestion costs and proposed solutions.

- In addition, a specific cost-benefit analysis was conducted, in two stages, for the proposed tourism development program. The result was an ERR of 17.3 percent. An overall economic assessment of the project was also made to estimate the mobilization of private resources as a result of investments by the public sector. The result was a robust leverage ratio of 1:3 after 15 years from project start, increasing to 1:5 in subsequent years.

- The increased land values attributable to new tourist itineraries were found to be sufficient to fully recover costs within a 10-year period with a 10 percent discount rate, even assuming a cost increase of 20 percent.

- Finally, a contingent value study was undertaken among tourists visiting Fès; another contingent value study was carried out among tourists visiting Morocco but not Fès; and a Delphi exercise was conducted in Europe among potential tourists. All of the resulting estimates, described in the project as "extremely conservative," showed very high economic benefits.

Cost-effectiveness analysis can be applied when benefits are deemed difficult to measure. As research in the economics of culture advances, new analytical procedures are being developed to put investments in CH on a sound economic and financial basis.

CHAPTER 4

World Bank Support for Cultural Heritage in the MENA Region

How has the World Bank responded to the challenges of preserving MENA's cultural patrimony? What are the strengths and weaknesses of the Bank's actual contribution? And what does the Bank's MENA region propose to do in the coming years?

1975–95: a brief retrospective on modest performance. The review of CH projects found that the Bank's contribution to CH in MENA during 1975–95 was modest. The Bank, in common with governments in the region, tended until recently not to consider patrimony management a significant area for development investments. (The 1980 decision to discontinue Bank lending for tourism contributed to the lack of interest.) The MENA region's policy statements, strategy papers, and country and sector work did little, if anything, to explore the congruence between this sector and poverty reduction strategies.[20] In turn, borrowing countries did not regard the Bank as a possible resource for CH protection. With rare exceptions, they did not submit their requests and project ideas in this domain to the Bank.

Over 20 years, only three projects in the MENA region included actual World Bank financing for the patrimony: Jordan Tourism I (1976), Egypt Luxor Tourism (1979), and Tunisia Urban Development III (1982).[21] (See Table 4.1.) Except in the Tunisia project, implementation efforts were weak, Bank commitment to supervision was inadequate, and performance (particularly in the Egypt project) was below standard. In hindsight, the Bank's support was not commensurate either with the importance of the region's patrimony or with the economic potential of its assets to contribute to countries' development agenda. Both the magnitude and the urgency of this sector's constraints were overlooked.

It must be noted that there were no policy obstacles to prevent the MENA region from doing much more along the lines of the three projects described above. Yet the concepts that governed lending programs

Table 4.1 MENA Operations in 1975–95 with Cultural Heritage/Tourism Components
(for amounts, millions of U.S. dollars)

Country	Project title	Bank	Approval date	Date effective	Closing date	Total cost	Ln/Cr amount for CH/CT[a]
Jordan	Tourism I	Cr. 06390	6/8/76	7/15/77	3/31/83	12.1	6.0
Egypt	Luxor Tourism	Cr. 09090	5/17/79	3/26/80	12/30/89	59.0	32.5
Tunisia	Urban Development III	Ln. 22230/s	12/16/82	9/8/83	6/30/93	60.1	25.0[b]

a. Ln./Cr., World Bank loan or credit. A considerable percentage of the loans was allocated for cultural heritage and cultural tourism (CH/CT). Percentages are based on a broad definition of CH/CT that includes improvements in visitor access to CH sites, on- or near-site visitor amenities and accommodations, and associated training and infrastructure services.

b. For the rehabilitation of a historic neighborhood: 22.8 percent of loan base cost.

Source: World Bank data.

and project design left the cultural domain out of development financing. Neither the Bank itself nor most borrowing governments connected investments for cultural heritage to the country's overall development program. In hindsight, the projects were happenstance investments responsive to occasional initiatives, rather than steps in a strategy. And investigation would probably show similar pictures for other regions.

1996–2001: patrimony support is growing. In the mid-1990s, the Bank's increasing commitment to improving its sociocultural impacts and environmental protection led to a renewed perception of cultural heritage issues. The last five to six years (1996–2001) have witnessed a demand-driven generation of innovative CH projects in the MENA region.[22] For the coming years, the question is how to further build on the beginnings of Bank work in this area. Analysis of the new CH projects in MENA—both ongoing and under preparation—reveals that they bring an array of creative approaches (Cernea 2001).

Central to the MENA region's orientation is the effort to mainstream the recognition of the sociocultural dimensions of development by taking them into account throughout its development agenda. As emphasized earlier in this paper, the MENA region works to address the sociocultural dimensions of development first of all at the level of every project intervention in all sectors (agriculture, urban, infrastructure, health, and others). Recently, the region has turned, more than in the past, to providing direct financial support as well, through projects focused on the culture sector per se, as well as through nonlending assistance.

Portfolio analysis shows that in terms of staff effort and material resources, the approach of incorporating cultural dimensions throughout the region's strategies and project interventions has been by far larger than that of making financial investments in distinct CH project interventions. This strategic balance is justified and should be maintained.

Direct investments in cultural infrastructure are currently channeled through four projects approved during 1997–2000: Jordan Tourism Development II, which includes cultural heritage preservation and management; Morocco Fès-Medina Rehabilitation, an urban rehabilitation project with considerable support for CH conservation; West Bank–Gaza Bethlehem 2000; and Yemen Second Social Fund for Development, designed to support small-scale community-based projects of various types, including CH-related projects. The MENA region has committed about US$80 million for these projects (see Table 4.2). Of this, about US$39 million, or 48 percent, is allocated directly for CH protection, management, and enhancement. Compared with total MENA

The Hafsia quarter of Tunis's old medina offers an early and successful example of including a historic city rehabilitation program in "regular" urban development programs, one of which was assisted by the World Bank. The program was financially profitable and restored Hafsia's livability, land and house values, and economic dynamism; it also earned the Aga Khan architectural award (1983).

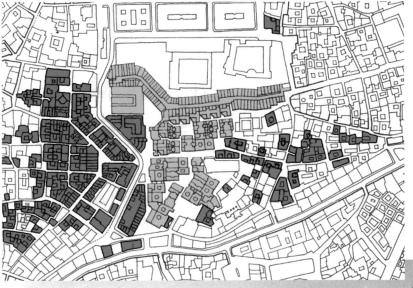

lending over the five-year period, this is still a relatively modest commit-ment, but it has allowed the start of policy dialogue about CH ground-work with a set of new institutions.

In addition, preparation of two new projects in the cultural sector in Lebanon and Tunisia is well advanced: Lebanon Cultural Heritage and Tourism Development, and Tunisia Cultural Heritage Management and Development. In 2000 the government of Morocco submitted a new request to the Bank for financing an urban development and heritage pro-tection project in Meknes, a historic imperial city on the World Heritage List. The preliminary parameters of these projects are shown in Table 4.3.

A remarkable initiative taken in 2000 was the introduction of finan-cial support for cultural heritage protection at the community level

TABLE 4.2

Current MENA Operations with CH Components, 1996–2000

(for amounts, millions of U.S. dollars)(for amounts, millions of U.S. dollars)

Country	Project title	Project ID	Approval date	Date effective	Closing date	Total cost	Ln/Cr amount
Jordan	Tourism Development II	PA 35997	1997	1997	2002	44	32
Morocco	Fès-Medina Rehabilitation	PE 5524	1999	1999	2004	27.6	14
West Bank– Gaza	Bethlehem 2000	SF 53985	1998	1999		25	25
Yemen	Second Social Fund		2000	2000	2005	75	9*

*Preliminary estimate. Amount may increase if adequate small scale projects will be identified and proposed by local communities.

Source: World Bank data.

TABLE 4.3

MENA Cultural Heritage Projects in Preparation

(for amounts, millions of U.S. dollars)

Country	Project title	Preappraisal	Appraisal	Preliminary total cost	Preliminary Bank Ln/Cr amount	Share of loan for CH/CT (percent)
Tunisia[a]	CH Management and Development	November 1999	September 2000	30	20	100
Lebanon	Cultural Heritage and Tourism Development	December 2001	March 2002	50[b]	30	60
Morocco	Meknes Cultural Heritage and Urban Dev.	2002	2002			

a. While this publication was being printed, the World Bank's Board of Executive Directors approved, on June 12, 2001, the loan for the Tunisia CH Management and Development project.

b. Includes US$30 million from the World Bank, US$10 million in donor cofinancing, and US$10 million in country financing.

Source: World Bank data.

through the Yemen Social Fund project, cofinanced by the Bank and other donors (Khan 2001). Several small-scale interventions have already been approved, and these will test the effectiveness of the approach for heritage management and poverty reduction, with a view toward further replication.

Looking at the Bank's overall CH portfolio in other regions, the projects approved in the MENA region are the largest investments in this domain, except for the China Yunnan Earthquake Reconstruction project. For instance, the Bank has US$39 million invested in the MENA region in its four ongoing projects, with an average of US$10 million per project. By comparison, US$24 million is invested in the Europe and Central Asia (ECA) region in 11 operations, of which 5 are institutional development fund grants and 6 are investment projects. The regional distribution of all Bank-assisted CH operations is shown in Table 4.4.

IFC tourism investments in MENA. Although not deliberately designed to address CH matters, the support provided by the World Bank Group through investments by the International Finance Corporation (IFC) in private sector hotel construction also contributes to facilitating cultural tourism. Between 1990 and 1999 the IFC approved 10 private hotel investment projects in the Middle East—in Egypt, Jordan, Lebanon, and West Bank–Gaza—as well as 2 in North Africa, in Morocco and Tunisia (see Table 4.5). Other investments are in

On the Tunisian island of Djerba, a candidate for UNESCO's World Heritage list, the La Ghriba Synagogue, founded here between 590 B.C and 71 C.E., and rebuilt several times, is one of the oldest and most important Jewish shrines in North Africa.

TABLE 4.4

Regional Distribution of World Bank–Assisted CH Projects

Region	Total	Projects Under implementation	Under preparation
MENA	7	4	3
Africa	3	0	3
ECA[a]	11	7	4
East Asia	6	2	4
South Asia	1	0	1
LAC	4	2	2
Total Bank	**32**	**15**	**17**

Note: ECA, Europe and Central Asia; LAC, Latin America and the Caribbean.

a. The total for the ECA region includes five institutional development fund grants of less than half a million dollars each. The number of projects Bankwide reflected in this table is continuously being revised and updated as new projects are prepared

Sources: ESSD, April 1999; MENA, January 2001.

preparation. As the private sector arm of the World Bank Group, the IFC lends in developing countries on a strictly commercial basis to private entities, not governments. It mobilizes substantial amounts of resources from private investors that can demonstrate the business case for a given project and that have the financial means to provide about 75 percent of the financing from non-IFC sources (Desthuis-Francis 2001).

Expanding hotel capacity for general purposes (business and leisure) increases visitor flows at heritage sites as well and helps capture more of the direct use value of cultural heritage. Yet this review found that some IFC tourism project documents tend to lack an explicit discussion of the cultural assets existing in the areas around the hotels and that possible adverse effects from increased visitor flows are not addressed through simultaneous protection measures for CH sites. This finding calls for closer cooperation within the Bank Group between MENA's Infrastructure Sector and the IFC on assistance to CH and tourism.

Nonlending assistance. In addition to lending, the MENA region also offers ongoing nonlending assistance for activities such as patrimony inventories (Yemen and Tunisia), strategy development (Tunisia and Morocco), museum development (Egypt), study programs and knowledge development (West Bank–Gaza), and special initiatives such as support for linking MENA handicraft industries with global markets through the Internet. (See the description in Box 4.1 of the "Virtual Souk," a Website for marketing traditional artisan products.)

Constraints on assistance. Although MENA's support for CH during 1995–2000 represents a substantial step forward compared with the previous two decades, it has been limited by several constraints. First among them was the absence of detailed country-based economic and sector work (ESW) devoted to the CH sector, which would normally precede Bank lending interventions. Similarly, the country assistance strategy papers (or their equivalents) for these countries had not explored the needs and potential of the CH sector.

MENA staff teams have made a sustained effort to overcome the ad hoc nature of those first interventions in Jordan, Morocco, and West Bank–Gaza. Nevertheless, regular ESW and CAS processes must, in the future, precede operations and provide the needed basis for them. Notwithstanding

TABLE 4.5

Current IFC Tourism-Related Projects in MENA

(millions of U.S. dollars)

	Project	$M
Egypt	Abu Soma Development Project	1.5
Egypt	Club Ras Soma Project	6.9
Egypt	Orascom Projects	24.8
Jordan	Business Tourism Co./ Marriott Dead Sea Project	5.0
Jordan	Jordan Inter-Continental	10.0
Jordan	Zara / Hyatt Amman, Dead Sea Movenpick	18.0
Lebanon	Idarat	11.5
Lebanon	Société Hotelier "Da Vinci"	3.0
Morocco	Credit Immobilier	17.3
Tunisia	Sousse-Nord	0.6
West Bank–Gaza	Jericho Motel	1.2
West Bank–Gaza	Palestine Tourism Investment/Jacir Palace	9.4
Total		**120.2**

Source: IFC data.

these limitations, some of the design solutions are pathbreaking for the Bank's support to CH. New options and ideas can be distilled from their pioneering experiences in preparing future comparable operations in other countries.

Strategic choices. In hindsight, what were the choices faced and the options adopted in these CH projects?

The initial strategic choice was among two possible project routes: either to design self-standing projects dedicated to the patrimony, or to design cultural components within investment projects in other lending sectors. Both routes are employed in the region. Projects in Jordan, Lebanon, and Morocco have taken the integrated component route; the project in Tunisia has taken the fully dedicated project route; and the West Bank–Gaza Bethlehem 2000 project is a combination of the two.

The component approach is able to capture the synergy between sectors—between urban development and cultural heritage, or between tourism facilitation and heritage conservation. It is also able to bring CH investments closer to the poverty reduction objectives pursued in each sector. Moreover, when institutional capacity in the country's cultural sector is weak, starting with a limited component may prudently build up capacity and models for subsequent larger-scale operations. In such cases, assistance to CH management was incorporated by using opportunities

BOX 4.1

The Virtual Souk: An NGO–World Bank Initiative

How can small handicraft producers break through the physical limits of their local markets and gain access to new customers?

A creative solution was developed in 1998 by NGOs in Tunisia and Morocco, with support from the World Bank Institute (WBI). To help Maghreb artisans use the Internet for selling internationally, they created the Virtual Souk (<www.elsouk.com>), a Website about North Africa and its culture.

Local artisans, who otherwise have little access to the international market, are now able through this Website to offer pottery, carpets, and wood, glass, and metal art products to the world at large, to state their prices, and to become more competitive. In turn, buyers' opportunities have expanded as well: they can bargain, communicate with the artists, make suggestions, and benefit from organized quality control.

The benefits from the Virtual Souk, and its differences from other Internet marketing services, are:

● **Income maximization for artisans.** The network of NGOs that manages the Website passes on all net income from sales directly to the artisans.

● **Decentralization to the cultural grassroots.** Outstanding local products are identified and promoted. Traditional arts and productive activities are revived and preserved at the grassroots, through market incentives.

● **Organizational capacity building.** International NGOs provide technical and commercial support to local NGOs and artisans. The WBI provides training in microenterprise management to local NGO personnel, who then offer training to the artisans.

The number of participating artisans has grown from 50 to about 1,000. Many of these producers have earned twice the incomes they did previously. The MENA region has helped to expand the Virtual Souk from Morocco and Tunisia to also cover Lebanon, Egypt, and Jordan. Moreover, the Bank's East Asia region is now replicating the Virtual Souk pattern in Thailand and other countries.

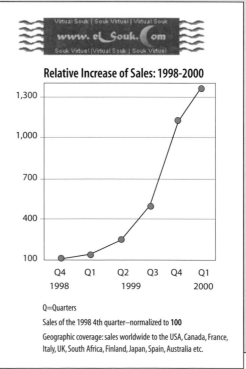

Relative Increase of Sales: 1998-2000

Q=Quarters

Sales of the 1998 4th quarter–normalized to **100**

Geographic coverage: sales worldwide to the USA, Canada, France, Italy, UK, South Africa, Finland, Japan, Spain, Australia etc.

inherent in various MENA projects to include CH components. In fact, the logic of the given project itself invited these components.

The following typology describes how such opportunities were used and converted into actual project components for CH support:

- The *urban improvement project* with a CH component is illustrated by the Morocco Fès-Medina Rehabilitation project. Because so many of MENA's heritage assets are located in urban settlements, links with urban infrastructure projects targeting urban poverty are indispensable. Project preparation broke new ground by crafting modern infrastructure solutions that would not damage the urban heritage, would mitigate pollution and congestion, and would introduce new institutional and financial mechanisms. The project will create 10,000 new jobs.

- *Cultural tourism* expansion is embodied in the Jordan Tourism Development II project, focused on Petra and Wadi Rum. This option builds on the inherent linkages between major patrimony assets and economically rewarding tourism. The project reverses the two-decade-long stagnation in tourism lending and also attempts to preempt the risks to CH entailed by increased tourist flows.

- *Post-conflict rehabilitation of patrimony* assets is exemplified by the Lebanon Cultural Heritage and Tourism Development project. Reconstruction that follows the calamities inflicted by wars and civil wars involves allocative and technical decisions for areas that may host enormously important heritage. Conventional wisdom holds that in a postwar situation the immediate needs are so many and pressing, and resources are so stretched, that hardly any financing can be found for culture and heritage. The Lebanon project, which supports major patrimony sites in the country's five largest towns, shows this conventional wisdom to be wrong. Ignoring heritage in post-conflict situations would be a sure recipe for making the wrong reconstruction decisions, soon to be regretted.

- *Institutional capacity creation* for CH was massively incorporated into the West Bank–Gaza Bethlehem 2000 project. In a patrimony rehabilitation intervention urgently required by the approaching millennial celebration, the Bank placed critical emphasis on capacity creation in an emerging country, helping build institutional structures from the ground up. An unusually high 40 percent of total project costs was allocated for institutional development. This approach lays the foundations for sustainability of future CH work. The poverty target group is about 100,000 Palestinians living in areas around the sites.

- The *national program* for CH support, embodied in the Tunisia Cultural Heritage Management and Development project and scheduled to begin in 2002, differs from the "component" approach. It is a full-scale, stand-alone CH support project, a more ambitious option not yet experimented with anywhere else in MENA or in other Bank regions. The government of Tunisia, after a long and mixed experience with piecemeal donor support for one or another of its historic monuments, concluded that it was in the country's best interest to adopt a national program. This approach consists of developing a countrywide strategy for CH preservation and management, defining criteria for site selection, and piloting the feasibility of each strategy objective on a suitably chosen site. Monitoring the pilot phase of the strategy will yield lessons for subsequent phases. Tunisia's relatively strong institutional and legal framework justified the adoption of this countrywide approach.

Worth noticing is that one option was avoided in the MENA region: *enclave projects* that focus only on one or several monuments, isolated from their context and intersectoral connections. Such enclave projects can achieve only a peripheral development impact.

Unsuccessful attempts. Not every MENA cultural project preparation effort, however, has been successful. In 1996 an attempt was made in Yemen to prepare a national cultural heritage project that would encompass strategy preparation, institution building, and CH rehabilitation works in Yemen's three historic sites on the World Heritage List, Sana'a, Shibam, and Zabid. The outline for project preparation, however, was not well thought through; it lacked selectivity and prioritization. It soon became obvious that a countrywide project would be overextended, given institutional weaknesses and limited implementation capabilities. The preparation process was inadequately monitored, and the consultant team failed to prepare any subproject for bidding and commencing work in time. The country management unit (CMU) therefore decided to stop preparation midway. This experience taught that countrywide programs through stand-alone projects can be realistically undertaken only when the needed prerequisites are created.[23] Alternative steps are being taken now to support small-scale CH activities through the Yemen Social Fund II project (2000) by defining eligibility criteria for Social Fund grants.

Addressing risks in a new sector. In undertaking project investments in a new area, MENA country and sector units have explored the risks that these new operations may confront. Such risk analysis should be carried out in the future, in every case. This sector review has ascertained that both risk analysis and the design of counterrisk measures are satisfactory in the CH projects described above. Beyond general investment risks, the risks specific to heritage projects that were identified explicitly are:

- *Tenure risks*, resulting from uncertainties about ownership over some heritage assets that require investments

- *Artistic risks*, related to the quality of conservation work and preservation of authenticity

- *Carrying-capacity risks*, or *congestion risks*, from precipitating low-quality, mass-market tourism that exceeds site capacities

- *Equity risks*, consisting in the diversion of benefits from CH investments away from the poverty target groups

- *Risks of unintended gentrification* through rehabilitation at the expense of driving poor families out of heritage areas

- *Cultural conflict risks*, resulting from biased, nonpluralistic approaches in CH preservation that may inflame ethnic or religious conflicts and instigate exclusion

- *Risks of population displacements and forced resettlement*, when undertaken to protect fragile sites

- *Risks of CH site encroachment* by people attracted by new economic opportunities.

Some of the risks specific to CH operations are relatively novel to the Bank. Therefore, the question has been asked: should the Bank stay away from these kinds of new risks and avoid altogether getting involved in CH operations? One of MENA's project appraisal documents directly answered this question by pointing to the opposite risk: the *risk of no action*, the risk of turning a blind eye to what happens to unprotected built heritage while doing "other" development operations (see Box 4.2).

Moderate risk levels. Overall, the sector analysis has found that the risk level in CH operations is moderate. Investments in CH do not increase the overall riskiness of projects, compared with other sectors. Specific risks, however, call for specific safeguards. In fact, CH operations emerge from the premise of preexisting high risks to the targeted CH assets and by definition are designed to reduce and eliminate these risks. Incorporating cultural components into projects in such sectors as urban infrastructure or tourism expansion has in fact proved functional as a "magnifying lens" for helping to identify project risks that might otherwise have escaped perception.

BOX 4.2

The "Risks of No Action" in Cultural Heritage

Weighing the risks of the Jordan Tourism Development II project against the risks of taking no action, the MENA staff concluded:

Not undertaking this project would result in several risks: (a) environmental degradation; (b) destruction of sensitive cultural heritage sites and landscapes; and (c) the irretrievable loss of tourist revenues. Because the project areas are susceptible to permanent damage solely from overuse, one of the major consequences of not undertaking the project would be the slow destruction of the very attributes that made these sites attractive in the first place. (World Bank Staff Appraisal Report, 1997, Annex 4, p. 2)

This comment is valid far beyond the confines of the project for which it was written.

Risk monitoring. The accuracy of the risk analyses made at project entry must be verified during implementation. Since the new MENA heritage projects are in their initial stages, it is too early to conclude whether additional risks, or higher intensities of anticipated risk, surface during implementation. An obvious shortcoming of the reviewed MENA projects, however, is the virtual absence of independent monitoring arrangements built into the projects and tailored to the characteristics of the cultural components and their economic and cultural objectives. Small monitoring units or independent studies can be introduced into projects currently in preparation, with scheduled project reviews at midterm.

Weaknesses in MENA's CH work. Besides revealing many accomplishments, the analysis of the past six years also identified several important weaknesses or avoidable difficulties in MENA's cultural heritage activities. These can be regarded as a compass for needed changes and improvements.

- *Lack of a strategic framework.* Recent lending for CH in MENA during 1996–2001 has taken place without the benefit of a specific regional strategy articulated in advance for the sector. Project initiatives have been taken as a result of country requests and have evolved in good part through the creativity of project staff, without the benefit of a pre-existing framework. The Fès-Medina project, for instance, started as a conventional urban infrastructure project and was reoriented ad hoc during preparation toward explicit CH preservation. It is a tribute to country officials and MENA staff working on the preparation of projects (e.g., those for tourism in Jordan and post-conflict reconstruction in Lebanon) that many linkages with CH were understood in mid-preparation and were incorporated into the design of projects.

- *Insufficient sector knowledge.* The ongoing MENA CH projects did not benefit from preliminary country ESW and, in fact, were ahead of the country strategy papers of the respective years, which had not envisaged these innovative interventions. Analysis of patrimony issues was absent from country strategy papers until 1999. Lack of holistic sectoral perspectives and priorities had to be at least partly compensated through longer-than-usual preparation work, constraining the sure-footedness and scope of the CH components. In the Tunisia case, for instance, the production of a sectoral strategy study was part of, rather than a basis for, the project preparation process.

- *Weaknesses in country data.* Although descriptive reports on the patrimony's deterioration and needs exist in abundance in every country, analyses of its economic potential (e.g., for poverty reduction in surrounding areas, job creation, and so on) are virtually nonexistent. Weaknesses in available country data and information gaps are characteristic constraints. With few and late exceptions, the Bank's MENA region did not commission specialized studies.

- *Insufficient policy dialogue with borrowers.* In the absence of ESW as a vehicle for dialogue, interaction with countries on CH has focused mainly on project issues, while broad strategy discussion has been insufficient. Such incomplete interaction has entailed inordinate delays and higher transaction costs in some projects.

- *Incomplete use of key Bank tools.* As a consequence of the lack of in-house coordination at the regional level, some Bank instruments adequate for the tasks at hand have never been used in MENA's CH work. Particularly conspicuous is that throughout the 1996–2001 period, MENA has not used the Bank's institutional development fund (IDF) grant window for CH, despite the need for institution building.

- *Overlooked educational implications.* As regards their content, MENA interventions to date have predominantly addressed infrastructural dimensions but have undertreated the educational aspects of CH management. Strikingly, none of the investment projects in the education sector processed between 1996 and 2000 in the MENA region attempt to promote the patrimony's contribution to education, pluralism, and identity cultivation through school programs or other means. The issue of education in indigenous languages has rarely been addressed.

- *Forgone opportunities and unevenness among sectors.* Opportunities to support CH were forgone in several sectors and projects (e.g., agriculture and rural development projects; environment projects). The Social Fund I project in Yemen, for instance, although eminently suited to support community-driven initiatives for safeguarding local assets, did not allow this option. (This limitation is corrected in the recent Yemen Social Fund II project.)

- *Failure to mobilize donor financing.* Although MENA had a major success in aid coordination for funding the Bethlehem 2000 project, there has been insufficient mobilization of donor financing to date for other projects (e.g., the Fès-Medina project). For some ongoing projects, this lacuna can still be corrected.

- *Inadequate staffing.* The expected addition of some specialists in patrimony management and cultural tourism to MENA staff has not yet materialized. The changing composition of staff/consultant teams employed to carry out preparation, appraisal, and supervision work on CH projects has led to lack of continuity, to ad hoc solutions, and to weaker review and analytical work. The absence until 2001 of an organizational focal point/staffing location in MENA for CH activities has weakened regional coordination.

- *Inadequate training.* The MENA region has offered only sporadic training opportunities on CH issues to its staff, except for the occasional seminars organized by the Bank's central group on culture and development. The World Bank Institute (WBI) has not developed specialized training modules for staff in this field.

Some of the weaknesses and difficulties discussed above are the typical growing pains of accessing a relatively new domain. If they are candidly recognized as shortcomings, the implications as to what needs to be done become obvious.

CHAPTER 5

MENA Strategic Priorities and Framework for Assistance

The findings of the CH sector review were discussed at a special meeting of MENA's Regional Management Team (RMT), which endorsed the analysis and adopted recommendations for carrying out and expanding further work in this domain (World Bank 2000). The strategic guidance offered by the RMT, the sequence of practical steps, and the instruments to be used are presented in this paper. This final chapter synthesizes the adopted recommendations into a regional framework for action and a work plan for the CH sector. The framework outlines what is to be done, in terms of key strategic and operational steps, to continue this work, expand assistance, and overcome the identified weaknesses.

What needs to be done? To respond to country demands for CH assistance, the first challenge to MENA region's staff is to bring CH work upstream in the process of defining country assistance. This involves shifting from discrete initiatives to (a) overall economic and sector work (ESW) and (b) CAS-level analysis for integrating the patrimony into national development strategies. To achieve this, partnership building is necessary. After the regionwide sector analysis, this will be pursued by moving toward holding country-by-country dialogues, workshops, consultations, and dissemination and toward country-based ESW. The purpose is to expand understanding and consensus and to identify priority needs and practical opportunities. The underlying premise is the integration of CH into mainstream development work, to better capture the patrimony's economic and noneconomic values for enhancing growth and development.

MENA's framework is based on the Bank's general policy of mainstreaming support to culture for sustainable development. It is integral, not parallel, to the region's overall development strategy.

In general terms, MENA's approach has two sides: (a) the pursuit of capacity-building strategic priorities and (b) immediate operational assistance and development of tools. The content of MENA's CH assistance will vary from country to country and is naturally adapted to local potentials and needs.

The need for sectorwide change. World Bank assistance to the CH sector would have its highest impact and justification if it benefited not just one or several location-specific projects, that is, piecemeal interventions in a country—important though these projects may be—but, rather, helped achieve sectorwide change. This is defined as positive impacts on all the constitutive elements of the CH sector (see Chapter I). Primarily, it would help bring about a major improvement in the institutional scaffolding of the sector. This is the essence of integrating the patrimony sector into the mainstream of country development and Bank-provided development assistance. Toward this goal, the present regionwide sector analysis has identified four long-term priorities for management capacity building for CH in MENA. Long-term work on ESWs and CASs will concentrate on the following four strategic priorities:

A. Policy definition and legislation updating

B. Institutional and organizational capacity building, including management decentralization

C. Civic engagement and multistakeholder participation in CH support

D. Financial reform, mobilization of nonbudgetary resources, and increased self-financing.

Strategic Priorities

1. Policies and Legal Frameworks

Policy development. The MENA region will provide assistance to member countries, when necessary, in the formulation of cultural heritage policies and of related legal frameworks. The central message promoted by the Bank (see Chapter II) is that a country's sectoral CH strategy needs to be linked to the country's central development and poverty reduction policy and reflect its general goals in ways specific to the cultural sector. Rather than being one-sidedly conservation oriented, CH policies serve best when they reflect not only what contemporary societies must do for the patrimony but also what the patrimony could do for the development of contemporary economies and societies. The use of cross-sectoral opportunities and the pursuit of intrasectoral and intersectoral synergies should become a policy cornerstone in each country.

Legislation. Updating and strengthening legal norms for effective safeguarding and sustainable CH management is indispensable. Legislation is integral to building up the countries' institutional capacity in culture, and the MENA region will contribute its share of technical assistance. The challenge is not to multiply indefinitely the number of regulations but, rather, to create a basic national legal framework, a code from which any other specific protective regulations (e.g., regulations on protecting CH assets under accelerated urbanization) will derive their legitimacy. Tunisia's *Code du Patrimoine*, for instance, is a possible model for such frameworks, which the MENA region can help replicate and adjust in other countries. The MENA region will also pursue the principle that improvements in CH legislation must be empowered by concordant education at the grassroots. To achieve increased civic awareness and internationalization of laws and regulations, intensified education and incentives for protection are indispensable.

2. Organizational Capacity and Reform

For not only preserving but also better managing their patrimonies, MENA countries critically need to create organizational capacity. Better institutional arrangements for making the patrimony endowments available to potential users (such as visitors, students, and inhabitants of historic buildings) can amplify the welfare created by the use of these assets. Appropriate organizations can maximize the difference between the costs and the benefits of CH preservation. The MENA region will primarily support reform to (a) enhance the state's central capacity, (b) decentralize authority and involve regional and municipal administrations, and (c) help establish specialized management organizations equipped with tools for modern public administration of the patrimony. Heritage management organizations ensure that places and practices in danger of disappearing will survive and will fulfill their economic and educational potential. These organizations do so by adding and enhancing the values of identity, exhibition, difference, and indigeneity (Kirshenblatt-Gimblett 1998). Since each country has specific national structures with different combinations of strengths, weaknesses, and needs, MENA staff must be equipped to consider these specificities.

Decentralization: central and local capacity. Since ownership of a large part of the material patrimony is vested in the state and most assets are public goods, it is essential to strengthen the capacity of the central institutions to which the state entrusts the responsibility of administration and management. In several MENA countries, the central institution is the ministry of culture, but differences exist, and in other countries responsibility for the archaeological patrimony is vested in the tourism ministry. Throughout the region, however, the central cultural organizations are weak. Ministries of culture in MENA countries tend to be among the least endowed government bodies in terms of financing, staffing, and equipment. They are also the least influential within the administration and receive little cross-sectoral support. This review concluded that, for performing their mandate as custodians of the nation's patrimony, ministries of culture (or equivalent departments) in MENA countries need additional expert resources and budgetary support. Studies of capacity characteristics and needs may be necessary.

Because in MENA countries the typical "central" CH institution is not yet a strong one, institutional capacity building in the CH domain must advance on two legs simultaneously: strengthening both the center (but without overcentralizing) and the periphery (the regions and municipalities). Decentralization (regionalization) of management, with adequate accountability, is in fact likely to strengthen the central CH institutions by unburdening them of part of their responsibilities and allowing them to concentrate on macropolicy and strategy management. Capacity creation includes empowerment of regional and municipal authorities, rather than exclusive central authority over pat-

Jordan: The famous temple carved into rock in the town of Petra, a World Heritage site.

rimony management.[24] Central state authorities are called on to create an enabling institutional environment for CH management throughout the country. The MENA approach maintains that the way to enhance local capacity and involvement is not exhortations but genuine devolution measures. Moreover, decentralized management is germane to the spatial distribution of the patrimony itself because assets are geographically scattered. Given the dual nature of patrimony ownership in MENA countries, where religious institutions own and manage a large segment of the national patrimony (see Chapter I, "Religious Institutions,"), state cooperation with these institutions is a prerequisite for success and for the effectiveness of MENA's assistance.

Cross-sectoral linkages. Regular intersectoral and interministerial cooperation is another strategic prerequisite for strengthening organizational capacity. The analysis in this paper has shown how essential it will be to overcome the gaps and the absence of partnerships between the several ministries whose activities relate to the country's patrimony. Specifically, this involves cooperation between the ministries of culture, of the Habous or Awqaf, of tourism, of urban development, of commerce and artisanat, of finance, and of the interior (or local administration). Ensuring better structural linkages is, of course, the responsibility of the respective governments. The MENA region's strategy will support and promote such cross-sectoral and interministerial linkages as an impact-multiplying mechanism that is indispensable for capturing the currently forgone synergies between culture and other sectors.

3. Civic Engagement and Multiactor Participation

MENA's triangulation approach. Given the nature of patrimony assets as public goods, the MENA region's CH strategy will pursue a *triangulated approach* in which the central role of the state is to be complemented by the contributions of the civil society and the private business sector in shouldering the responsibilities of preserving the heritage and transmitting it to future generations. Ranging from grassroots communities to middle-class and upper-middle-class strata, massive engagement in CH preservation by the civil society is indispensable because patrimony assets will only be safeguarded if this goal is championed by every collectivity. However, the propensity for engaging in militant protection and maintenance does not emerge spontaneously, in the absence of education, and should not be assumed as a given.[25] MENA will recommend the triangulated approach to countries as a long-term strategic priority, while operational interventions will further translate triangulation into operational arrangements. NGOs, state and privately sponsored museums, local associations, women's organizations, professional societies, and many other structures can take on heritage preservation as an explicit cause, becoming devoted custodians of local patrimony assets while deriving economic and educational benefits for themselves. The MENA region proposes to help empower such trends.

Engaging the business sector. The business sector has essential interests in the patrimony's uses and controls significant resources. There are instances in which the private sector can offer more material support than the state can provide, while some segments of the business sector also have interests that may at times conflict with heritage sustainability. Making business aware of its responsibilities and inviting its due contribution should therefore be seen as a strategic goal.[26]

4. Financial Reform and Self-Financing

Budgetary constraints. In preparing CH interventions, examining the financial underpinnings of a country's patrimony should be a preliminary step for the MENA region. This review has revealed a considerable disequilibrium between the importance of the sector for a nation's existence, the pressing needs for the patrimony's preservation, and current budgetary allocation levels. Many benefits generated by the existence of CH are produced in the patrimony sector, but in practice, these benefits are being captured and accounted for in other sectors, such as tourism. That distorts intersectoral financial transfers and reduces the incentives and resources for improving CH management. The MENA region will provide analytical support to countries for optimizing financing patterns and, as necessary, can help in designing sectoral financial reform in the context of the Bank's macroeconomic work.

Increased self-financing and voluntary contributions. There are at least three avenues for supplementing the budgetary CH resources by resorting to other sources: increasing self-financing, mobilizing voluntary donations, and seeking external grant aid. Patrimony preservation can pay for itself to a larger extent than it currently does if management and financial mechanisms are modernized. Revised pricing systems for visitors and for various cultural services will help capture enhanced revenues. Tax incentives and moral stimuli may go a long way toward mobilizing contributions from the business sector and private citizens, thus alleviating the burden on the state. The MENA region will systematically assist countries in mobilizing grants and concessional aid from bilateral and multilateral donors, using cofinancing arrangements and an array of other instruments.

Bank investment assistance. To assist in financing, the Bank itself can continue CH investment assistance for MENA countries and increase it above 1995–2000 levels, if borrowing governments ask for such assistance and the activity supports CAS diagnoses. The Bank's regional development strategy views such financial support to CH primarily as seed investments necessary to activate the sector's underused potentials, rather than large-scale, bulky investment loans. Seed investments are most appropriate for financing the opportunities for CH components in various projects, testing new approaches, and creating premises for more significant follow-up investments.

Operational Steps

Lending and nonlending support. Explicit guidance for translating the four strategic priorities defined above into both lending and nonlending assistance has been provided by MENA's Regional Management Team (RMT) and is explained below. Several specific forms of assistance are outlined.

Criteria for MENA's CH lending. For its decisions, the MENA region will use the same transparent lending criteria as does the Bank at large, adjusted to circumstances in the region. Whether the MENA region will support a specific investment in a CH project will depend on the project's expected economic and noneconomic impacts and on the Bank's comparative advantage. Drawing on Board-approved criteria, lending for CH support will be evaluated in terms of how it:

- Reinforces sectoral or project objectives or core development activities

- Reduces poverty and stimulates employment and enterprise by the poor

- Strengthens institutional and managerial capacities in the cultural sector, including the development of national CH legislation and strategies

The traditional Harad stone and alabaster oil lamps of various shapes, used in Yemen and in other parts of the Middle East, are today largely replaced by electricity but will perennially testify to times past.

- Contributes to the heritage-related formation of social capital and to education

- Leverages private direct investments, multiplies secondary benefits to the poor, and yields tax revenue

- Helps promote revenue-generating cultural tourism

- Contributes to protection of the heritage and the environment against risks of deterioration and irreplaceable losses

- Adds value to assistance from other donors.

Conversely, the MENA region will *not* finance culture-based activities when:

- There is not a demonstrable socioeconomic gain consistent with the Bank's development mandate and poverty reduction objectives.

- Alternative financing from other international organizations, particularly grant financing, is available and sufficient.

- Such lending is not consistent with the CAS or does not rest on an effective demand by the borrowing country.

The MENA region will continue to implement the Bank's long-standing policy of not financing projects, in any sector, that will damage nonreplicable cultural heritage. Early in the project cycle, staff will review the possibility of such adverse impacts. (Appropriate preventive measures may include change of project area, project redesign to fully preserve a site, site protection measures, selective salvage and data recovery, and site data recording.) The region will also avoid "monumentalism" and will not finance enclave projects that focus only on conserving one or several discrete monuments in isolation from their sociodemographic and economic surroundings.[27] Projects that focus narrowly on conservation will not fit into the MENA lending framework because restoration without site management is unsustainable, and economic values are captured by improving management, not through conservation only. Furthermore, MENA will not finance archaeological excavations, which are highly specialized activities and are best organized, financed, and managed by academic institutions and grant aid. How-ever, after excavations and research are completed and the site is considered safe for regular visitation and tourist activities, Bank assistance may be provided to improve access facilities (such as transportation, roads, and accommodations to integrate the site into tourist circuits). The value added of MENA assistance comes primarily from enhancing the impact of good patrimony management towards overall socioeconomic development.

Country dialogue. To implement these lending criteria, and following up on the sector analysis, MENA staff will engage in dialogue with countries' relevant agencies to identify the highest-priority cultural needs. Careful case-by-case judgment is required for efficient use of Bank resources in a development-oriented mode. Selectivity, partnerships, and leveraging of the Bank's comparative advantages remain crucial.

Nonlending assistance. As it has done in recent years, the MENA region will continue to provide nonlending assistance in various forms to support CH preservation, inventorying, and management. Nonlending support activities may be initiated either as parts of projects or as distinct activities in the country programs. Bank nonreimbursable grants in the form of institutional development funds (IDFs) may be extended in support of policy development, institutional reform, and studies for project preparation. The nonlending assistance should not be a "dead-end" activity but should, rather, aim at preparing the ground for subsequent programs. However, the prospect of a subsequent project is in no way a condition for nonlending assistance.

Cross-sectoral versus stand-alone projects. The sector study concluded that MENA's experiences to date, its innovations, and lessons from past weaknesses offer a solid basis for a diversified range of project vehicles, designs, and instruments for CH lending and nonlending support. Within this range, two basic models can be used:

- *Cross-sectoral projects with a CH component.* These are development projects that support various noncultural sectors which, by their content and location, may naturally include assistance for patrimony assets in their area. This model will take advantage of, rather than forgo, the windows of opportunity that appear frequently in other sectors' projects. It will facilitate integration of CH concerns into mainstream development programs and build up new cross-sectoral as well as interministerial operational links. An additional consideration is that components are in many ways simpler to prepare.

- *Stand-alone cultural projects for patrimony support.* These encompass the sector's activities in a broader way than a component. This pattern appears justified where the country's institutional framework in the cultural sector is stronger or when preliminary activities have prepared the ground for a broader program. Depending on its size, the self-standing project can be either a regular investment project or a smaller-scale learning and innovation loan (LIL) project. When conditions are appropriate, programmatic lending can be provided through a series of successive projects of broadly the same kind through the Bank's new adaptive program lending (APL).

At the current stage, when experience and management capacity in the patrimony sector are still limited, the first of the two models appears more adequate, easier to implement, and likely to involve lower transaction costs. The stand-alone project is practicable only in special, appropriate circumstances. To decide which model to use in a given situation, MENA staff will apply the following transparent criteria: (a) the nature of the country's request to the Bank and other country considerations, (b) the available opportunities and resources, and (c) institutional strength in the cultural sector.

Project content. Within cross-sectoral approaches, CH provisions will differ from sector to sector. The spectrum is broad. The sectors in which projects may lend themselves best to the inclusion of CH components are urban infrastructure, tourism development, agriculture, postconflict reconstruction, environment, and education and human resources. Content elements for project packages suitable for the circumstances in MENA countries are suggested below.

- *Urban development projects* can aim at supporting rehabilitation work in medinas to achieve a triple impact—added jobs, improved services and living standards, and salvaging of urban architectural assets under threat. Such projects can improve road networks around medinas and service roads inside old towns to facilitate economic revitalization. They can also relocate out of the medinas the polluting industries that adversely affect the inhabitants and damage patrimony assets.

- *Agricultural and rural development projects* can be designed to incorporate components for preserving local CH assets in rural zones, thus stimulating nonagricultural employment; support community-driven initiatives such as community-based museums and visitation sites; support folk art; and assist in integrating rural heritage areas into touristic circuits, opening up opportunities for incubating small businesses and reducing rural poverty.

- *Tourism sector projects* can link investments in tourism infrastructure expansion to improvement of patrimony management; promote cross-sectoral linkages between cultural tourism and all related cultural enterprises (primarily handicrafts); increase grassroots communities' benefits from culture-based tourism in and around those communities; and help build institutional capacity specialized in organizing cultural tourism.

- *Industry and microcredit projects* can include components supporting the handicraft industry, based on cultural traditions and folk arts; help reorient the culture-based handicraft industry away from cheap, low-quality products toward high labor inputs and high-quality, high-value, high-priced items, thus absorbing more employment and increasing marketability; and enable the establishment of various new small and medium-size cultural enterprises in the private sector.

- *Education and human resources projects* can aim at incorporating knowledge about the national patrimony into school curricula and instilling a culture of heritage custodianship; cultivating public awareness and helping create "social fencing" for patrimony protection; and promoting formal functional linkages between schools, museums, and archaeological sites, for using the latter as educational platforms.

- *Environment projects* can include protective and preventive measures to safeguard historic cultural assets from imminent natural hazards; help relocate polluting industries that damage patrimony assets; and support establishment of parks for unique cultural and biosphere sites.

The content packages outlined above are flexible and can be used within a wide range of project opportunities. Other elements may be identified as well. MENA staff will work with relevant country agencies to determine the available options and select the most promising. The task ahead is not to mechanically incorporate culture-support activities when the linkages are not organic with what is the core of one or another sector's project. It is, rather, to customize project design and incisively grasp and exploit the genuine windows for synergy when the use of such opportunities enhances development impacts in both sectors.

Full-scale culture support projects. Some governments may be interested in Bank support for large-scale, freestanding CH projects. The MENA region could finance such projects (as in Tunisia) when it ascertains that there is already institutional capacity in the country to undertake more complex projects or after a preliminary activity (including nonlending assistance) that builds the capacity for stand-alone patrimony-focused projects.

The place of CH in broad national strategies. Another macrostrategy option consists of formulating issue-centered national strategies within which the patrimony can play a special role in a "compact" with several other related sectors. An example of such a national strategy might be a special *employment promotion* strategy to address the fundamental problem of unemployment, which reaches levels of over 10–20 percent in some MENA countries. Within such national employment expansion strategies, support for CH would open avenues for additional job creation in the service sectors.[28] The ability to link, cross-sectorally, CH management to regular activities in other sectors under their respective development projects is a clear expression of the Bank's comparative advantage and of the value added that it contributes.

Learning and innovation loans (LILs). Other relatively new project vehicles, such as LILs and APL, can also be employed for CH support. *Learning and innovation loans* provide loans of up to US$5 million based on regional management decisions, without requiring a Bank Board lending decision. As their name indicates, LILs are designed for learning new lessons from innovative approaches while minimizing the risks of financial exposure. LILs are adequate when a country prefers to test new approaches to CH preservation, capacity building, and management on a small scale and move rapidly to implementation.[29]

Adaptive program lending (APL). The structure of the patrimony also lends itself to the use of *adaptive program lending*. Medinas in North Africa, for instance, are "units of the patrimony" that share many common characteristics. This makes possible replication and the adaptation, in stages, of the approach initially tested in one medina to others with comparable needs. The methodology used initially can be refined at each subsequent program stage. This ensures a program approach, rather than a discrete, piecemeal approach. It facilitates continuity, transfer of experience, and the development of a core transferable staff with tested skills. It also reduces transaction costs and project preparation time for both the country and the Bank.

Nonlending assistance. Financial investments can be paralleled by various nonlending assistance activities. In response to borrowers' requests, MENA will be prepared to provide nonlending support along the following lines:

● Support for the elaboration of country policies or strategies in the CH domain, synchronized with the country's overall development and poverty reduction objectives.

● Inclusion of CH-specific provisions regarding management goals in CDFs, CASs, poverty reduction strategy papers (PRSPs), public expenditure reviews (PERs), and other analyses.

- Assistance for CH institutional capacity building or institutional reform, as a contribution to better patrimony management.

- Support for financial reform, when needed, to improve the current ineffective financing arrangements for patrimony administration. Such reform will increase self-financing and financial sustainability. It will be based on detailed financial analysis of the sector, linked to the Bank's country macroeconomic work.

- Provision of nonrefundable resources through an institutional development fund (IDF) or the Development Grant Facility (DGF), for a clear cultural sector action program.

- Studies for preparing CH preservation, management, and marketing activities.

- Assistance for establishing national registries and inventories of patrimony, particularly if requested in connection with bilateral grants for such projects.

- Mobilization and coordination of donor cofinancing for CH.

Mosaic recently discovered at the Jabalia Church in Gaza, during civil works for a Bank-assisted development project.

Project Preparation Instruments

Investment projects in CH preservation and management will be subject to the same robust economic, social, and environmental analysis as all Bank-assisted projects.

Economic and financial analysis. Because heritage assets, as public goods and objects of culture, realize their economic and educational functions in specific ways, instruments tailored to estimate their cost-benefit ratios or cost-effectiveness are necessary. Both market and nonmarket valuation techniques have been designed for this purpose. Among these economic analytical procedures are the hedonic price method, the contingency valuation method, and the travel cost method.[30] These tools have been used in recent MENA projects for the economic and financial analysis of the Morocco Fès-Medina Project (see Box 3.3, above), as well as in projects under preparation such as the Lebanon CH project and the Tunisia Cultural Heritage Management and Development project.

The use of these techniques is described in detail in the project appraisal documents (PADs) for these projects and represents a good model for replication in future comparable MENA operations. Analytical methodologies for this domain are continuously being refined.

MENA project economists and financial analysts are working to introduce such improvements in practice and to put these projects on a sound economic and financial basis.

Social and environmental assessments. Forthcoming MENA operations in the cultural sector will involve ex-ante, in-depth social assessments and environmental assessments tailored to the content of the sector.

Social assessments are demanded for this category of investments, given the cultural nature of patrimony assets and the need for civic engagement in their preservation. Social analysis in project preparation and appraisal is needed not just for a passive, descriptive assessment but also for the proactive design of sociocultural provisions germane to the project's substance. The social preparation of such projects must analyze the issues that have been addressed in this review, such as maximizing development impacts, institutional capacity, pluralism in preservation, risks to the built patrimony, the mechanisms and incentives for civic engagement, and particularly the role of local communities in the custodianship of patrimony assets. Special terms of reference will need to be designed for social and cultural analysis, focused also on preventing adverse impacts from physical environmental factors and from exceeding carrying capacities for tourist visitation.

The MENA region will continue to require borrowers to assess impacts on cultural resources in projects proposed in all sectors that are located in a known heritage site or that involve excavations, demolition, flooding, or other environmental changes. Screening, scoping, and onsite inspection of physical cultural resources will provide the information needed to include adequate protection and management provisions in project design.[31]

Risk analysis. Concern for high quality in culture-support projects requires the identification, preemption, and mitigation not only of general project risks but also of risks specific to the nature of these operations. Projects in the CH domain, in fact, *start* from the perception of risks, since support activities are needed precisely because the given assets already face multiple risks of deterioration and disappearance. Risk analysis specific to CH should focus on risks resulting from uncertain tenure over some cultural assets; risks from cultural bias, sectarianism, and nonpluralistic approaches; possible risks to the quality of restorative works; risks from the uninformed behavior of populations living near CH assets; and risks of unwarranted resettlement or of inequitable distribution of benefits.

Strengthening In-House Capacity

To expand its assistance in the CH domain, and to implement the conclusions of this sector analysis, the Bank's MENA region needs to strengthen its current in-house capacity. Recent work has produced several well-designed operations but has also revealed the mark of ad hoc, insufficient preparation or follow-up and the need for better internal staff coordination and resourcing. An action plan for in-house work has been prepared that includes measures for organizational strengthening, staffing, training, studies, donor coordination, publication, dissemination, and so on.

Country dialogue and knowledge generation. First and foremost, the MENA region will carry out a large-scale effort to raise awareness about the findings of the sectoral analysis and its strategic and operational recommendations. One or two regional conferences of countries in the Mediterranean basin, including both developing and donor countries, will be organized to examine opportunities for cooperation in CH preservation and management. MENA's country teams will initiate dialogues with interested governments, using the present sectoral review and recent experiences as a basis for exploring countries' immediate and long-term needs, constraints, and priorities, donor collaboration, and specific assistance actions. A program of country-focused ESW and other studies, with support from the Italian Trust Fund for Culture and Sustainable Development (ITFCSD) and from other sources and Bank partners, will be initiated to develop the in-depth knowledge necessary for work on specific country programs. Such studies will explore further ways of deriving cultural and economic benefits with tangible impacts on poverty reduction from CH investments. Studies on pricing of cultural services and self-financing will develop new solutions for sectoral financial reform. Institutional audit studies will inform the capacity-building assistance and develop a knowledge base for future operations.

Dialogue with donor organizations. The MENA region will move from ad hoc contacts with bilateral and multilateral donors to a program of regular contacts and consultations in CH work. Country-focused consultations with other donors on cofinancing issues will be scheduled at the request of the interested government. Arrangements for a consultative forum, which would meet every two years, will be explored with UNESCO, UNDP, the European Union, and other interested international and bilateral donors.

Looking ahead. At the threshold of the third millennium, this strategy framework looks toward the prospects for preserving the extraordinary MENA cultural heritage of worldwide importance and for making possible the Bank's contribution to it. The past is prologue. The patrimony is both foundation for the present and a building block for developments in the future. Forthcoming generations are entitled to receive their ancestors' cultural heritage well safeguarded and to fully enjoy it.

Notes

1. According to UNESCO's operational guidelines for the WHL, a site nominated for the list may be one that is a "masterpiece of human creative genius" or "bears a unique . . . testimony to a cultural tradition" or is "an outstanding example" that illustrates a significant stage or significant stages in human history.

2. This decision has been corrected in practice, through the resumption of the Bank's assistance for tourism development, particularly during the second half of the 1990s.

3. Statement by Willem M. Van Haarlem, archaeologist and leader of the multinational scientific team conducting the excavations at Tel Ibrahim Awad (see *Washington Post*, April 4, 2000).

4. For details on the privately owned and exemplarily endowed and managed Musée Belghazi in Salé-Rabat, see Abdelilah Belghazi (1999).

5. Tunisia's Agence de Mise en Valeur du Patrimoine et de la Promotion Culturelle exists parallel to the country's policy and research institute devoted to the patrimony.

6. The ministry of culture usually includes within its structure a department of antiquities that is in charge of material-heritage matters—mainly conservation, inventorying, and excavations—but not of the mise en valeur, public use of and access to patrimony assets

7. In Yemen, for instance, culture and tourism are under one ministry, and the Department of Antiquities is in the cultural part of the ministry; Egypt has two different ministries, Culture and Tourism. In Jordan, the Department of Antiquities is attached not to the Ministry of Culture but to the Ministry of Tourism and Antiquities (MOTA), while the other cultural departments are in the Ministry of Education. The Palestinian Authority has included a unit for archaeology in its Ministry of Tourism.

8. It is noteworthy that during consultations held in preparing this review, country governments agreed with this assessment and in fact often volunteered it, signaling capacity constraints and asking for Bank assistance with CH institution building.

9. A significant step was taken in Tunisia in 2000 when the sector's share was raised to almost 1 percent of the budget.

10. The World Bank's Operational Directive 4.20, on Indigenous People (1989) covers the recognition, demarcation, and protection of indigenous people's lands and the provision of culturally appropriate social services. The revisions introduced in the late 1980s strengthened the initial policy by stressing the cultural uniqueness of indigenous groups and the need to promote the informed participation of the indigenous people, and their right to share in the benefits of development projects, and to emphasize the cultural uniqueness of indigenous groups.

    Operational Policy Note 11.03, on the Management of Cultural Property in Bank-Financed Projects, is in the process of conversion, but it remains effective until the Board has reviewed the new text. See also Goodland and Webb (1987).

11. The consideration of sociocultural variables in other development interventions is illustrated by a variety of well-known MENA activities and approaches. It is reflected, for instance, in the increasing use of social analysis in MENA project preparation through social assessments, poverty assessments, gender analysis, and so on; the increased weight of MENA lending for social development sectors such as human resources, social funds, and social protection; the efforts to involve the civil society in defining development priorities and programs; and the increased proportion of participatory approaches. All these have created a propitious context for addressing CH issues as well.

12. ICOMOS, based in Paris, is the International Council on Monuments and Sites; ICCROM (Rome) is the International Centre for the Study of the Preservation and Restoration of Cultural Property; and ICOM (Paris) is the International Council of Museums. The CJA (Center for Jewish Art) is part of Hebrew University, Jerusalem.

13. Caveats to this statement concern the fragility of some heritage goods and the risks of congestion, that is, of exceeding carrying-capacity limits, as discussed in Chapter IV.

14. In support of the MENA sector strategy on cultural heritage, David Pearce and Susana Mourato (University College London) prepared a synthesis of the research on CH economic valuation methodologies. The synthesis offers a comprehensive assessment of the state of the art in this domain and will be published separately (Pearce and Mourato forthcoming) to guide the detailed economic analysis work for preparing CH investment projects.

15. See Dixon, and others (1994); Pagiola (1996); Pearce and Mourato (1998).

16. In April 2000, Development Economics (DEC), Economically and Socially Sustainable Development (ESSD), and the Poverty Reduction and Economic Management Network launched a research program on the relationship between culture and the Bank's core mandate of sustainable poverty reduction (Walton 2000; see also Alkire, Rao, and Woolcock 1999).

17. In connection with valuation, the concept of cultural capital has been introduced by cultural economics specialists to facilitate adaptation of concepts such as investment, depreciation, rates of return, and differentiation between stock and flow to the area of heritage preservation. Throsby (1997: 17) offers a definition of cultural capital:

We might define cultural capital specifically in the context of immovable heritage as the capital value that can be attributed to a building, a collection of buildings, a monument, or more generally a place, which is additional to the value of the land and buildings purely as physical entities or structures, and which embodies the community's valuation of the asset in terms of its social, historical, or cultural dimension. Cultural capital, like the physical capital in which it is contained, can have its asset value enhanced by investments in its maintenance or improvement. The social decision problem in regard to this type of cultural capital might be seen within the framework of social cost-benefit analysis. Ranking projects according to their social rate of return (and) decision-making in this area . . . could utilize the familiar mechanics of investment appraisal. The appropriate rate of return is that which takes account of both *tangible* financial flows and of *intangible* effects arising as public goods or beneficial externalities.

18. Such valuation techniques are widely used for environmental evaluation and are also increasingly used by governments and by the World Bank in the culture heritage sector.

19. Neither the World Tourism Organization nor individual countries generally disaggregate tourism data by category (e.g., "beach tourism," "cultural tourism"; some tourists may be in both categories). Tourism specialists, however, tend to have informal estimates for each category.

20. Exceptions include activities related to implementing the 1986 Operational Policy Note (OPN 11.03) on chance cultural finds in areas of Bank-financed projects.

21. Some tangential, very limited support was also included in the Egypt Private Sector Tourism Infrastructure and Environmental Management project (1993).

22. A detailed description of these ongoing activities is offered in the full MENA CH sector analysis study (World Bank forthcoming); see also Cernea (2001).

23. The Bank now provides nonlending assistance to Yemen's cultural sector, managing the work on a national CH inventory financed through a grant from the government of Italy. The Bank is also exploring the feasibility of creating a trust fund for CH preservation work (Brizzi 2000).

24. Two options for such decentralized capacity, in light of the experiences of MENA and others to date, can be contemplated:
    • The creation of *subcentral entities* at the regional horizon, between the center and the municipalities, vesting in them area management and project implementation (e.g., the Petra Regional Council and the Aqaba Regional Authority, in the Jordan Tourism Development II project)
    • The creation of capacity in *municipalities*, enabling them to run preservation and management activities for local historic sites (e.g., the Morocco Fès-Medina project).

25. In fact, as emphasized previously, much deterioration of the built heritage unfortunately results from neglect, indifference, or the harmful activities of those who ought to be the most immediate protectors of the heritage.

26. Morocco's successful initiatives in mobilizing *le Mécénat* illustrate the practical feasibility, and the effectiveness, of this strategy element.

27. This does not imply that such monument-focused restoration work is not justified for other agencies. On the contrary, various circumstances may sometimes require that work of this kind be undertaken with great urgency—for instance, for salvage reasons. Other specialized organizations, however, are better equipped than the Bank to carry out such activities.

28. An example will illustrate this possibility more clearly. As noted in Chapter III, Morocco's former Ministry of Tourism proposed to increase the number of foreign tourists from 2 million to 4 million as a goal of the country's 2000–2010 development plan. This objective is impressive. However, a review of the ministry's plans reveals an obvious disconnect between goal and means. Few cross-sectoral partnerships with the Ministry of Culture and other ministries are planned, and there is a high risk that, despite good intentions, the objective will not be reached. Morocco's unemployment rate is about 20 percent of its labor force, with urban youth unemployment at around 31 percent. Absorbing as much as possible of this mass of unemployed persons is crucial. The case can be made that a broader cultural tourism/cultural heritage (CT/CH) compact that would include the infrastructure, artisanal, and transportation sectors would make the goals of moving from 2 million to 4 million tourists and of absorbing a significant segment of the unemployed much more achievable. This, however, would not be a strategy for the Tourism Ministry and the tourism sector alone, or for CH alone, or for infrastructure or any other sector alone. What is needed is a *multisectoral, integrated, mainstream development strategy* that brings together improved preservation and management of the patrimony; development of highways, access roads, and hotel infrastructure for wider cultural tourism circuits; expanded air, bus, and rail transportation; expanded handicraft production and markets; and broad incubation of new small and medium-size businesses to provide the secondary and tertiary services needed to support a doubled tourist flow. Comparable compacts may be pursued in some other countries in the region, with appropriate adjustments. The growth benefits of such a potential macrostrategy are indisputable. This is relevant to the sector analysis because the CH sector is pivotal to such growth. The Bank can provide essential assistance in pursuing such a development route.

29. Some governments may be reluctant to use LILs because they are small yet entail about the same transaction costs and complex domestic procedures (for example, parliamentary approval) as larger loans. In such cases, larger-scale, free-standing projects tend to be considered.

30. Pearce and Mourato (forthcoming) discusses the economic methodology for assessing investments in culture support projects. The paper explains the application of valuation techniques and economic and financial analytical methods, verified in MENA and elsewhere, to forthcoming CH projects.

31. See World Bank, OP 4.11, Physical Cultural Resources (draft, February 2001).

References

Al Abboudi, Nassir H. 1994. "United Arab Emirates Museums." In International Council of Museums (ICOM), *Musées, civilisations et développement*. Amman.

Abdelilah Belghazi, Mohammed. 1999. "Communication." In *Culture Counts: Financing, Resources and the Economics of Culture in Sustainable Development*. Washington, D.C.: World Bank and UNESCO.

Abouseif, D. B. 1994. "Reconnaissance Report of Damages to Historic Monuments in Egypt, following the 1992 Dashour Earthquake." State University of New York, Buffalo.

Al-Far, Darwish Mostafa, Ibrahim Tavaar Al Jabar, and others. 1994. "The Qatar National Museum and other Qatari Museums." In International Council of Museums (ICOM), *Musées, civilisations et développement*. Amman.

Alkire, Sabina, Vijayendra Rao, and Michael Woolcock. 1999. "Culture and Development: From Theory to Operational Relevance." World Bank, Poverty Reduction and Economic Management, Washington, D.C. Processed.

Al-Rfou'h, Faisel. 1999. "Remarks on the Role of Culture in Sustainable Development." In *Culture Counts: Financing, Resources, and the Economics of Culture in Sustainable Development*. Washington, D.C.: World Bank and UNESCO.

Al-Sindi, Khalil Mohammad. 1994. "Preservation and Restoration Work at the Laboratories of the Bahrein National Museum." In International Council of Museums (ICOM), Musées, civilisations et développement. Amman.

Amahan, Ali. 1999. *Héritage cultural; au Maroc* Study commissionsed by the World Bank. Rabat, Processed.

Amahan, Ali. 1997. *Mutations sociales dans le haut Atlas*, Ed. Maison des sciences de l'homme, Paris, Ed, La Portem Rabat.

Berriane, Mohamed. 1997. *Tourism, culture et développement dans la region arabe*. October. Rabat, UNESCO. Processed.

Bouabdellah, Malika. 1994. "Le rôle et les objectifs d'un musée national en Algérie." In International Council of Museums (ICOM), *Musées, civilisations et développement*. Amman.

Braudel, Fernand. 1966. *The Mediterranean and the Mediterranean World in the Age of Philip II*, vol. 2. New York: Harper & Row.

Brizzi, Gianni. 2000. "Proposal for a Cultural Heritage Trust Fund." Memorandum. September. World Bank, Washington, D.C.

Cernea, Michael M., ed. 1991. *Putting People First: Sociological Variables in Development Projects*. New York: Oxford University Press.

————. 2001. "At the Cutting Edge: Cultural Patrimony Protection through Development Projects." In Ismail Serageldin, Ephim Shluger, and Joan Martin-Brown, eds., *Historic Cities and Sacred Sites: Cultural Roots for Urban Futures*. Washington, D.C.: World Bank.

Cernea, Michael M., and Chris McDowell, eds. 2000. *Risks and Reconstruction*. Washington, D.C.: World Bank.

Commission on Global Governance. 1995. *Our Global Neighborhood*. Oxford, U.K.: Oxford University Press.

Crocci, Giorgio. 1997. *Studies on Seismic Vulnerability of Minarets in Cairo and Criteria for Improving Their Safety*. Universita degli Studi di Roma.

Dervis, Kemal, and Nemat Shafik. 1998. "The Middle East and North Africa: A Tale of Two Futures." *Middle East Journal* 52 (4, autumn): 505–16.

Desthuis-Francis, Maurice. 2001. "Investment Impacts of Tourism in Historic Districts." In Ismail Serageldin, Ephim Shluger, and Joan Martin-Brown, eds., *Historic Cities and Sacred Sites: Cultural Roots for Urban Futures*. Washington, D.C.: World Bank.

de Wulf, Luc. 2001. "Yemen: Budget and Institutional Reform in Support of the Five Year Plan." Draft. February. World Bank, Middle East and North Africa Economic and Social Department, Washington, D.C. Processed.

Dixon, John A., Louise Fallon Scura, Richard A. Carpenter, and Paul B. Sherman. 1994. *Economic Analysis of Environmental Impacts*. 2d ed. London: Earthscan.

Fey, Bruce S. 1997. "The Evaluation of Cultural Heritage." In Michael Hutter and Ilde Rizzo, eds., *Economic Perspectives on Cultural Heritage*. London: Macmillan; and New York: St. Martin's Press.

Goodenough, Ward. 1987. "Multiculturalism as the Normal Human Experience," in Elisabeth Eddy and William Partridge, eds., *Applied Anthropology in America*. New York: Columbia University Press.

Goodland, Robert, and Maryla Webb. 1989. *Management of Cultural Property in World Bank–Assisted Projects: Archaeological, Historical, Religious, and Natural Unique Sites*. World Bank Technical Paper 62. Washington, D.C.

Gugliotta, Guy. 2000. "Dig Offers a Rare Peek at 'Pre-Dynastic' Egypt." *Washington Post* (April 17): A09.

Hutter, Michael, and Ilde Rizzo, eds. *Economic Perspectives on Cultural Heritage*. London: Macmillan; and New York: St. Martin's Press.

Ibrahim, Wahid, and Rachid Ghorbel. 1995. "Rapport de le Commission sur la promotion du Tourisme Culturel." Tunis. Processed.

ICCROM (International Centre for the Study of the Preservation and Restoration of Cultural Property). 1996. "Synthèse de l'enquête sur le patrimoine culturel maghrébien." Draft. April. Rome.

ICOM (International Council of Museums). 1994. *Musées, civilisations et développement*. Amman.

IMF (International Monetary Fund). Various years. *Government Financial Statistics*. Washington, D.C.

IRCICA (Research Centre for Islamic History, Art, and Culture). 1999. "The First International Seminar on Traditional Carpets and Kilims in the Muslim World: Past, Present, and Future Prospects for Developing This Heritage in the Context of Continuous Changes of the Market Design, Quality, and Applied Techniques, November 1999, Tunis." Istanbul, Turkey.

Johnson, Peter, and Barry Thomas. 1990. "Measuring the Local Employment Impact of a Tourism Attraction: An Empirical Study." *Regional Studies* 24: 395–403.

Kaul, Inge, Isabelle Grunberg, and Marc A. Stern, eds. 1999. *Global Public Goods: International Cooperation in the 21st Century*. New York: Oxford University Press.

Khan, Qaiser M. 2001. "Yemen Final Fund for Development and the Preservation of Cultural Heritage." March. Processed.

Kirshenblatt-Gimblett, Barbara. 1998. *Destination Culture: Tourism, Museums, and Heritage*. Berkeley, Calif.: University of California Press.

Maarouf, Nazeih. 1999. *Awards of the First International Islamic Artisans-at-Work Festival*. Catalogue of winning entries at the festival held in Islamabad, October 1–14, 1994. Istanbul, Turkey: IRCICA (Research Centre for Islamic History, Art, and Culture).

Melikian, Souren. 1997. "The Destruction of Art and History in Iran and Afghanistan." Paper presented at the Symposium on the Anthropology of Cultural Heritages, School of American Research, Santa Fe, N. Mex.

Mitchell, H., and Tunisian National Tourist Office. 1995. *Etude de l'aide de l'Etat au secteur touristique*. 3 vols. Tunis, SETEC Economic.

Mourato, Susana. 1997. "Effects of Air Pollution on Cultural Heritage: A Survey of Economic Valuation Studies." Report prepared for the UN Economic Commission for Europe. Centre for Social and Economic Research on the Global Environment (CSERGE), University College London. Processed.

Narkiss, Bezalel. 2001. "Synagogue-Church-Mosque," in Ismail Serageldin, Ephim Shluger, and Joan Martin-Brown, eds., *Historic Cities and Sacred Sites: Cultural Roots for Urban Futures*. Washington, D.C.: World Bank.

Navez, Françoise. 1995. "Projet de sauvegarde de la Médina de Fez." April. Report to the World Bank. Processed.

Pagiola, Stefano. 1996. "Economic Analysis of Investments in Cultural Heritage: Insights from Environmental Economics." World Bank, Washington, D.C. Processed.

Pearce, David, and Susana Mourato.1998. "Economic and Financial Analysis for Cultural Heritage Projects." Centre for Social and Economic Research on the Global Environment (CSERGE), University College London. Processed.

————. Forthcoming. "Economic and Financial Analysis for Cultural Heritage Projects. Valuation Methods and Techniques." MENA Economic Working Paper Series. World Bank, Washington, D.C.

Rypkema, Donovan D. 1998. "Preservation as Economic Generator in the US: Cultural Resource Preservation and Economic Development." USPS, Washington, D.C.

Sarbib, Jean-Louis. 2000. "Minutes of the MENA Regional Management Team Meeting." World Bank, Washington, D.C.

Serageldin, Ismail. 1990. "Architecture and Behaviors: The Built Environment of the Muslims," in Suh Ozkan, ed., *Faith and the Built Environment: Architecture and Behavior in Islamic Culture*. Lausanne, Switzerland.

Serageldin, Ismail, Ephim Shluger, and Joan Martin-Brown, eds. 2001. *Historic Cities and Sacred Sites: Cultural Roots for Urban Futures*. Washington, D.C.: World Bank.

Tagemouati, Naima Lahbil. 1999. *Patrimaine, tourisme et emploi*. Cas du sud du Maroc. Study commissioned by the World Bank. Rabar Processed.

————. 2001. "Mére et fille en Medina." Fés, Moroc: Editions Le Fennec.

Throsby, David. 1997. "Seven Questions in the Economics of Cultural Heritage." In Michael Hutter and Ilde Rizzo, eds., *Economic Perspectives on Cultural Heritage*. London: Macmillan; and New York, St. Martin's Press.

UNESCO (United Nations Educational, Scientific, and Cultural Organization)/ Palestinian Authority. 1998. "Bethlehem 2000 Emergency Action Plan for the Bethlehem Area." Synthesis report. West Bank–Gaza. Processed.

UNESCO, World Heritage Committee. 2000. "Periodic Reporting: Report on the State of Conservation of World Heritage in the Arab Region." Presented at the 24th Session of the World Heritage Committee, Cairns, Australia, November 27–December 2. WHC-2000/CONF.204/7. Paris. Summary available at <http://www.unesco.org/whc/toc/mainf15.htm>.

van Eeghen, Willem, and Jennifer Keller. 1999. "Workers in Crisis in the MENA Region: An Analysis of Labor Markets Outcomes and Projects for the Future." World Bank, Middle East and North Africa Social and Economic Department, Washington, D.C. Processed.

Walton, Michael. 2000. "Culture and Poverty: Call for Research Issues from Operations." Office Memorandum. World Bank, Poverty Reduction and Economic Management, Washington, D.C.

Wolfensohn, James D. 1997. *The Challenge of Inclusion*. Address to the Annual Meetings of the World Bank and the International Monetary Fund, Hong Kong, September 23. Washington, D.C.: World Bank.

————. 1999a. "Foreword." In "Culture and Sustainable Development: A Framework for Action." World Bank, Environmentally and Socially Sustainable Development, Washington, D.C.

————.1999b. "A Proposal for a Comprehensive Development Framework." Memorandum, January 21. World Bank, Washington, D.C. Available at <http://www.worldbank.org/cdf/cdf-text.htm>.

World Bank. 1997. "Jordan: Tourism Development II Project." Project Appraisal Document. Washington, D.C.

————. 1999a. "Culture and Sustainable Development: A Framework for Action." Environmentally and Socially Sustainable Development, Washington, D.C.

————. 1999b. "Morocco Fès-Medina Rehabilitation Project." Project Appraisal Document. Washington, D.C.

————. 2000. "Minutes of the MENA RMT Meeting of September 6, 2000." Washington, D.C. Processed.

————. Forthcoming. *Cultural Patrimony and Development: Approaches and Experiences in the Middle East and North Africa Region.* Directions in Development series. Washington, D.C.

Maps

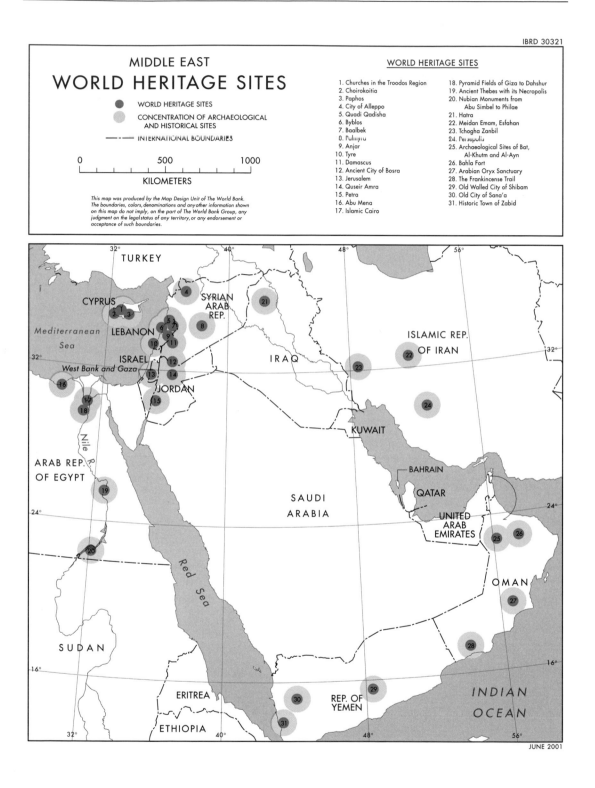

IBRD 30321

MIDDLE EAST
WORLD HERITAGE SITES

● WORLD HERITAGE SITES

○ CONCENTRATION OF ARCHAEOLOGICAL
  AND HISTORICAL SITES

—·—·— INTERNATIONAL BOUNDARIES

0   500   1000

KILOMETERS

This map was produced by the Map Design Unit of The World Bank.
The boundaries, colors, denominations and any other information shown
on this map do not imply, on the part of The World Bank Group, any
judgment on the legal status of any territory, or any endorsement or
acceptance of such boundaries.

<u>WORLD HERITAGE SITES</u>

1. Churches in the Troodos Region
2. Choirokoitia
3. Paphos
4. City of Alleppo
5. Quadi Qadisha
6. Byblos
7. Baalbek
8. Palmyra
9. Anjar
10. Tyre
11. Damascus
12. Ancient City of Bosra
13. Jerusalem
14. Quseir Amra
15. Petra
16. Abu Mena
17. Islamic Cairo

18. Pyramid Fields of Giza to Dahshur
19. Ancient Thebes with its Necropolis
20. Nubian Monuments from
    Abu Simbel to Philae
21. Hatra
22. Meidan Emam, Esfahan
23. Tchogha Zanbil
24. Persepolis
25. Archaeological Sites of Bat,
    Al-Khutm and Al-Ayn
26. Bahla Fort
27. Arabian Oryx Sanctuary
28. The Frankincense Trail
29. Old Walled City of Shibam
30. Old City of Sana'a
31. Historic Town of Zabid

JUNE 2001

IBRD 30322

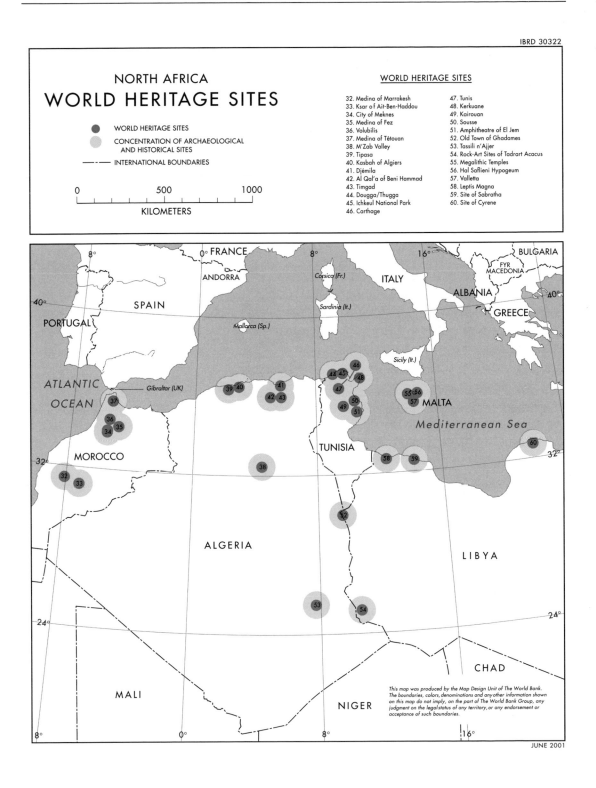

NORTH AFRICA
WORLD HERITAGE SITES

● WORLD HERITAGE SITES

● CONCENTRATION OF ARCHAEOLOGICAL
  AND HISTORICAL SITES

–·–·– INTERNATIONAL BOUNDARIES

0   500   1000
KILOMETERS

WORLD HERITAGE SITES

32. Medina of Marrakesh
33. Ksar of Ait-Ben-Haddou
34. City of Meknes
35. Medina of Fez
36. Volubilis
37. Medina of Tétouan
38. M'Zab Valley
39. Tipasa
40. Kasbah of Algiers
41. Djémila
42. Al Qal'a of Beni Hammad
43. Timgad
44. Dougga/Thugga
45. Ichkeul National Park
46. Carthage

47. Tunis
48. Kerkuane
49. Kairouan
50. Sousse
51. Amphitheatre of El Jem
52. Old Town of Ghadames
53. Tassili n'Ajjer
54. Rock-Art Sites of Tadrart Acacus
55. Megalithic Temples
56. Hal Saflieni Hypogeum
57. Valletta
58. Leptis Magna
59. Site of Sabratha
60. Site of Cyrene

This map was produced by the Map Design Unit of The World Bank.
The boundaries, colors, denominations and any other information shown
on this map do not imply, on the part of The World Bank Group, any
judgment on the legal status of any territory, or any endorsement or
acceptance of such boundaries.

JUNE 2001

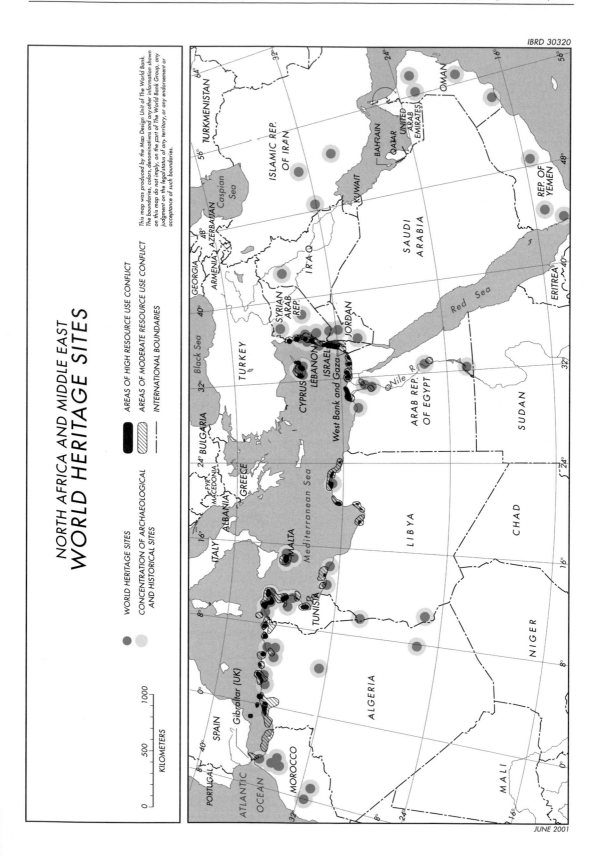

IBRD 30320

NORTH AFRICA AND MIDDLE EAST
WORLD HERITAGE SITES

WORLD HERITAGE SITES

CONCENTRATION OF ARCHAEOLOGICAL
AND HISTORICAL SITES

AREAS OF HIGH RESOURCE USE CONFLICT

AREAS OF MODERATE RESOURCE USE CONFLICT

INTERNATIONAL BOUNDARIES

This map was produced by the Map Design Unit of The World Bank.
The boundaries, colors, denominations and any other information shown
on this map do not imply, on the part of The World Bank Group, any
judgment on the legal status of any territory, or any endorsement or
acceptance of such boundaries.

KILOMETERS

0   500   1000

JUNE 2001

Illustration Credits

ILLUSTRATION CREDITS

Cover photo: Mosaic of the Jabalia Basilica, Gaza, Photography: Courtesy of Ministry of Tourism, Palestinian Authority.

Page 5: United Arab Emirates: Iron age pots. Photography: Courtesy of the Embassy of UAE, Washington, D.C.

Page 6: Morocco, Marrakesh: Koutoubia Mosque, ongoing repair (top); Fès: Medrassa Es Sahrij: Photography: Michael M. Cernea. Jordan- Roman ruins at Jerash (bottom). Photography: Ekaterina Massey and Mohammed Feghoul.

Page 10: Morocco, Volubilis. Photography: Michael M. Cernea.

Page 13: Syria, Palmyra. Roman Theater: Khanassar Valley: Beehive houses. Photography: Ruth Cernea.

Page 15: Morocco, Fès: Brass artisan. Yemen, Sana'a area: Silver belt. Photography: Michael M. Cernea.

Page 18: Syria, Damascus: Umayyad Mosque. Photography: Michael M. Cernea.

Page 23: Saudi Arabia, Jeddah: Old houses. Photography: Michael M. Cernea.

Page 25: Algeria, Algiers: The Kasbah. Photography: Dominique Roger, courtesy of UNESCO Collection.

Page 26: Egypt, Luxor: Statue of Ramses II. Photography: Nenadovic, courtesy of UNESCO Collection. Syria, Damascus: Dura Europos Fresco. Photography: Courtesy of The Center for Jewish Art.

Page 27: Syria, Bosra. Roman amphitheater. Photography: From the Ministry of Tourism, Syria.

Page 28: Iran, Isfahan: Grand Shah Mosque. Photography: Courtesy of Aga Khan Trust for Culture.

Page 32: Morocco, Essaouira: Ramparts, city walls. Photography: Ruth Cernea.

Page 35: Tunisia, Sidi Bou Said village. Photography: Michael M. Cernea.

Page 37: Yemen: Jewelry. Photography: Michael M Cernea.

Page 40: Egypt, Cairo: Photography: Courtesy of the Aga Khan Trust for Culture.

Page 45: Morocco, Volubilis: Triumphal Arch. Photography: Ruth Cernea.

Page 47: Syria, Damascus: Whirling Dervish. Photography: Ruth Cernea.

Page 50: Yemen, Sana'a: The Souk. Photography: Michael M. Cernea.

Page 53: Tunisia, Tunis. Photography: Courtesy of Restaurant Dar El Jeld.

Page 54: Yemen, Shibam. Photography: Michael M. Cernea.

Page 56: Yemen, Old Sana'a Architecture. Photography: Michael M. Cernea.

Page 59: Tunisia, Hafsia: City Plan map, Harvard School of Design. Photography: Mona Serageldin.

Page 61: Tunisia, Djerba: La Ghriba Synagogue. Photography: Ruth Cernea.

Page 67: Morocco, Essaouira: Doorway. Photography: Ruth Cernea.

Page 74: Jordan, Petra: Temple in the Rock. (Historic Cities and Sacred Spaces, World Bank).

Page 77: Yemen/other Middle East countries: Stone oil lamps. Photography: Michael M. Cernea.

Page 83: Gaza. Mosaic, The Church at Jabalia. Photography: Courtesy of Ministry of Tourism, Palestinian Authority.